Quiet·Fire

EMILY
DICKINSON'S
LIFE AND
POETRY

Twenty-First Century Books™
An imprint of Lerner Publishing Group, Inc.
241 First Avenue North
Minneapolis, MN 55401 USA

For reading levels and more information, look up this title at www.lernerbooks.com.

Illustrations on pp. 9, 83, 88–89 by Laura K. Westlund.
Main body text set in Adobe Garamond Pro.
Typeface provided by Adobe Inc.

Library of Congress Cataloging-in-Publication Data

Names: Dommermuth-Costa, Carol, author. | Landsverk, Anna, author.
Title: Quiet fire: Emily Dickinson's life and poetry / Carol Dommermuth-Costa, Anna Landsverk.
Description: Minneapolis: Twenty-First Century Books, [2022] | Revised edition of: Emily Dickinson (Minneapolis, Lerner Publications, 1998). | Includes bibliographical references and index. | Audience: Ages 11–18 | Audience: Grades 7–9 | Summary: "Emily Dickinson is revered as one of America's greatest and most original poets. Quiet Fire presents the life and art of Dickinson through the poet's own letters and poems"—Provided by publisher.
Identifiers: LCCN 2020021292 (print) | LCCN 2020021293 (ebook) | ISBN 9781728416342 (lib. bdg.) | ISBN 9781728416359 (eb PDF)
Subjects: LCSH: Dickinson, Emily, 1830–1886—Juvenile literature. | Poets, American— 19th century—Biography—Juvenile literature.
Classification: LCC PS1541.Z5 D59 2022 (print) | LCC PS1541.Z5 (ebook) | DDC 811/.4—dc23

LC record available at https://lccn.loc.gov/2020021292
LC ebook record available at https://lccn.loc.gov/2020021293

Manufactured in the United States of America
1-48884-49201-11/11/2021

TABLE OF CONTENTS

INTRODUCTION

The summer of 1886 was a grim time in Amherst, Massachusetts. Lavinia Dickinson's sister was freshly in the ground. Vinnie, as her family called her, had the unfortunate task of sorting through her dear sister's belongings. Most of the possessions were no surprise—several stark white cotton dresses, piles of letters carefully marked for either burning or sharing with family, and a beloved book collection. But what Vinnie did not expect to find was a trunk filled with nearly two thousand scraps of paper and tightly bound homemade notebooks. That wealth of paper was covered in poetry in tight, hard-to-decipher handwriting. Vinnie's discovery would not only upend her sister's reputation in their small New England community but also shake up American literature for centuries to come.

Only after Emily Dickinson's death did her sister discover the poet's substantial collection of poems.

Everyone close to Emily Dickinson knew she was a poet, but they had no idea of the scope of her work. She frequently enclosed poems in letters to family, friends, and people whose work she respected. Emily even sent poems folded in neat rectangles next door to her brother Austin's house to share with him and his wife (Emily's longtime close friend), Susan. Still, the writer kept much of her work to herself, scribbling alone in the upstairs bedroom of her childhood home. Only in death would Emily reveal some of her secrets; many others, she took to her grave.

Most writers aim to be published authors and poets. But Emily had a more complicated relationship to public attention. She dedicated a number of poems to fame and its implications for those trapped in its web. One such poem uses a cheeky persona, or poetic voice, to make fun of those who look for recognition, comparing them to noisy frogs looking for mates. It reads,

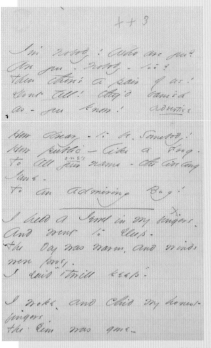

"I'm Nobody! Who are you?" is one of Emily Dickinson's most famous poems.

> I'm Nobody! Who are you?
> Are you - Nobody - too?
> Then there's a pair of us!
> Dont tell! they'd advertise - you know!
>
> How dreary - to be - Somebody!
> How public - like a Frog -
> To tell one's name - the livelong June -
> To an admiring Bog!

Whether to her joy or dismay, Emily Dickinson is far from nobody. Her life and work continue to be revered, researched, and reinvented by readers young and old. Her unique poetic style has inspired countless writers, and her air of mystery has captured the imaginations of creators the world over.

ONE

I'M NOBODY! WHO ARE YOU?

1830–1839

Amherst, Massachusetts, in the mid-nineteenth century wasn't much to look at. The small community had only a few general stores, a church, and the aptly named Amherst College. Farming and agriculture dominated the landscape. Many families grew their own vegetables and fruit. Some even raised chickens and cows for eggs, cheese, and milk. Most kitchens had a pump for water, but outdoor privies were still the norm. The bookstore carried several newspapers and only those books considered by the community to be good, wholesome reading. Most of Amherst's under five thousand citizens built their homes on one of two streets: Main Street or North Pleasant Street. There were no railroads until 1853, so most people traveled in small, two-wheeled carriages known as cabriolets. They used candles and gas lamps to light their homes and streets. The townspeople needed little from the outside world.

The Dickinson family had lived in Amherst for generations. By the nineteenth century, the Dickinson name was ubiquitous in the small community. Emily's grandfather, Samuel Fowler Dickinson, had been one of the supporters of Amherst Academy, which Emily would eventually attend. He also helped found Amherst College in 1821. The college consisted of two buildings with dormitories where students from out of town could live while completing their courses.

Samuel Fowler Dickinson drove the college's creation at times by force of will alone, often taking on the financial risks of the new project himself to keep construction going. His blind determination did see the college built, but Emily's grandfather struggled for years to keep Amherst College open, let alone financially stable. By 1830 he was on the verge of bankruptcy. Amherst College almost closed that year.

To conserve money, the Dickinson family all moved in together. They lived in a large red brick house on Main Street called the Homestead. Samuel Fowler Dickinson his wife, Lucretia; and their younger children lived in one half of the house. His son Edward; his wife, Emily Norcross Dickinson; and their first child, William Austin Dickinson, lived in the other half, which was separated by a common hallway

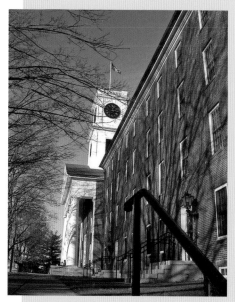

College Row at Amherst College

and stairs leading to the second floor. Emily Elizabeth Dickinson was born in the Homestead on December 10, 1830.

A comfortable white porch supported by four huge columns ran along the front of the Homestead. A barn sat on the property, as well as a shed for the family carriage and a huge woodpile to fuel the stove and fireplace. On the side of the house there were apple, pear, cherry, and peach trees; a vegetable garden; and a beautiful flower garden.

Unfortunately, in the middle of all the beauty at the Homestead, a great deal of turmoil existed when Emily was a baby. Her grandfather, bankrupted by the financial strain it took to keep Amherst College open, was forced to give up the fight. In 1833, when Emily was two years old, Samuel Fowler Dickinson took his wife and their two youngest children and moved to Cincinnati, Ohio. Emily's grandfather would never again live in Amherst or see the schools he gave up so much to establish.

Edward Dickinson was just starting his practice as a lawyer. He barely made enough money to support a large house and a family. He was also burdened with the financial responsibility of supporting his brother Frederick along with Frederick's wife and two children. This financial

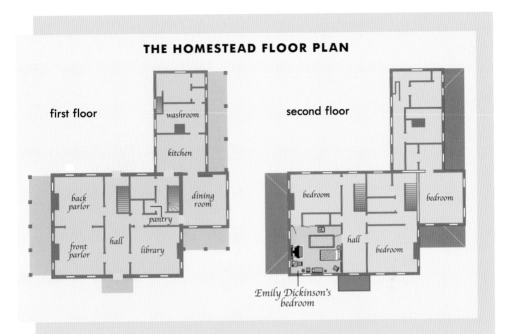

THE HOMESTEAD FLOOR PLAN

first floor

washroom

kitchen

back parlor

dining room

pantry

front parlor

hall

library

second floor

bedroom

bedroom

bedroom

hall

bedroom

Emily Dickinson's bedroom

pressure filled the whole household with anxiety. The shame of Edward's father leaving for Ohio also made it difficult for Edward to recoup valuable social status in the eyes of the Amherst upper-class community.

Then Emily's mother, Emily Norcross Dickinson, found that she was expecting a third child. She was very sick and couldn't care for both three-year-old Austin and two-year-old Emily. Emily Norcross Dickinson asked her sister Lavinia if Emily could live with her for a while. So Emily was sent away to stay with her aunt, who lived about 30 miles (48 km) from Amherst.

Aunt Lavinia wrote to Edward Dickinson about her young niece:

> Emily is perfectly well and contented — She is a very good child & but little trouble — She has learned to play on the piano — she calls it the *moosic* She does not talk much about home — sometimes speaks of *little Austin* but does not moan for any of you — She has a fine appetite & sleeps well & I take satisfaction in taking care of her. . . .
>
> I took her to meeting yesterday morning — She behaved very well — Once in a while she would speak loud but not to disturb

Samuel Fowler Dickinson built the Homestead in 1813. He owned it for twenty years before selling it to David Mack, a general store owner in Amherst. When Mack died in 1855, Edward Dickinson purchased the property and moved his family back into the house. Emily Dickinson spent much of the last twenty-five years of her life on the property.

any one — she sit between Pa & me — he would slap her a little occasionally when she was doing wrong — not to hurt her or make her cry —

During this period, Emily was happy and content to bask in the affection of her aunt. As short and early in Emily's life as the time was, the poet would remember it fondly for years after. After a year with her aunt, Emily was returned to her home. Her younger sister, Lavinia, had been born, and her mother had recovered enough to care for all three children.

However, this did not mean Emily's mother could give her daughter the same level of interest the young girl had gotten from Aunt Lavinia. The lack of attention and affection was very difficult for Emily. This change was likely part of what prompted Emily to say years later, "I never had a mother. I suppose a mother is one to whom you hurry when you are troubled."

There was a disconnect between mother and daughter on more than just attention, though. Emily Norcross Dickinson was well educated, but only for the purpose of better raising her children and caring for the house. She put most of her energy into keeping an efficient home and being a hospitable hostess to her husband's clients and guests. Even before she and Edward were married, Emily Norcross's letters do not exhibit the same gushed excitement about learning that her daughter's correspondence does. Instead, she is reserved, short, and hesitant.

Emily never thought of her mother as a woman of education. She saw her as a quiet, frail woman who seemed to have little time or desire for intellectual pursuits. Emily Norcross Dickinson often suffered from ill health, usually brought about by her husband's long absences from home. Edward Dickinson had to travel to Washington, DC, a great deal as a lawyer and politician, and when he was away for more than a week, Emily's mother became very depressed and took to her bed.

Even though Edward showed little affection toward his children, Emily adored her father. When he was home, he read the Bible to Austin, Emily, and Vinnie every morning and led them in their prayers every night. He was very strict and set in his ways. Emily rarely saw him smile, and his tone of voice could be gruff and impatient. When he was unhappy with something Emily said or did, he would show his displeasure with stony silence. Even so, Emily missed him when he was away. In a letter to her husband, Emily's mother expressed how much his children, particularly Emily, missed their father:

January 21, 1838 . . . The children are well except Emily she has not been as well as usual, for a week I think however she is much better now. I have not let her go to school more than two or three days since you left. She speaks of her Father with much affection. She sais she is tired of living without a father.

Soon Emily had other pursuits to occupy her time. In 1835, when Emily was four years old, she started school in a two-story whitewashed

A FATHER ON DAUGHTERS: EDWARD DICKINSON ON WOMEN'S EDUCATION

Before he had two daughters, Edward Dickinson had strong beliefs about the roles of women and girls in society. In 1827 he submitted five essays to the *New-England Enquirer* about "Female Education." He used the pen name Coelebs, Latin for bachelor, after the name of a character in a book that emphasized how practicing traditional feminine skills prepared women for wife- and motherhood.

Under the protection of anonymity, Edward Dickinson dismissed the idea that women's education could be beneficial for them or for society at large. He explained that while women might have learning capacities equal to men, the last thing a man wanted to come home to was a wife who would discuss lofty philosophical, scientific, or literary theories. Education unrelated to a woman's domestic duties as wife and mother was wasted, as it would not help her get the household work done. Edward also condemned women who often went out to parties or events, instead insisting women should be at home whenever possible.

The Coelebs essays were written while Emily Norcross and Edward Dickinson were courting through letters. Some scholars have suggested that Edward was hoping to influence the woman he wished to marry into better fitting his image of the ideal woman. He also openly told Emily Norcross in the many unanswered letters he sent that she should forgo parties and public events. For her part, the young bride-to-be did not budge. She sent back short, terse responses or no response to many of his letters. But after three years of courting, she agreed to Edward's marriage proposal, and his dreams of having a wife that matched his criteria were realized.

Even in conservative 1820s Amherst, Edward Dickinson's essays struck a nerve. Townspeople decried such an extreme position on women's education and called for the newspaper not to print all of Edward's essays. The editors relented. But despite the unpopularity of his opinion, Edward did not waver. True to his essays, he restricted Vinnie and Emily from going out, marrying, or engaging in public events after they reached their teen years. Edward cast a long shadow over his daughter and her ability to believe in herself as a valued, intelligent individual with plans outside the Homestead's walls.

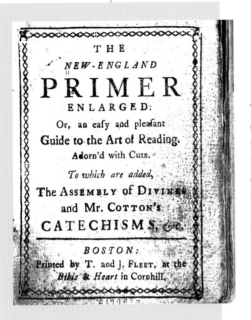

The *New-England Primer* was originally published in the seventeenth century and was the first reading primer designed for the American colonies. While there was some variation in the text over the years, the book always included standard reading concepts, including the alphabet, vowels, consonants, and double letters.

brick building on Pleasant Street. The students all used the same textbook, *The New-England Primer*, which taught them not only to read and write but to live a good Christian life so they could enter heaven when they died. Emily learned to read from this book, which was filled with prayers and religious rhymes. She had to memorize the prayers and say them regularly. One of the bedtime prayers taught Emily that there was a connection between sleeping and death:

> I in the burying place may see
> Graves shorter there than I:
> From death's arrest no age is free—
> Young children too may die.
>
> My God, may such an awful sight
> Awakening be to me!
> O! that by early grace I might
> For death prepared to be!

It was unusual in 1835 for a girl of Emily's age to attend school. But

DICKINSON POETRY 101:
HOW TO READ EMILY'S WORK

One of the features of Emily Dickinson's poetry that made it remarkable was how unusual it was for her time. However, those same features can make her work challenging to read even now. To make it easier, here's a cheat sheet on reading Dickinson.

Of particular annoyance to her early editors was Emily's refusal to title her poems. Perhaps this was because the poems were never explicitly intended for publication, or perhaps she just didn't like titles. Either way, because there are no titles, there are a few different ways people reference her poetry. The first method is to refer to her poems according to their opening line. To use a well-known example, "'Hope' is the thing with feathers" is how one would refer to this poem:

> "Hope" is the thing with feathers -
> That perches in the soul -
> And sings the tune without the words -
> And never stops - at all -

This method is often used to index collections of Dickinson's poetry for easy reference. It's also handy for looking up poems online. However, in articles and analysis of her poetry, writers will also sometimes use numbers to refer to Dickinson's works. These numbers correspond to the chronological order of her poems as guessed at by two prominent Dickinson scholars. The first of those scholars is Thomas Johnson, the first person to publish a full collection of Dickinson's poetry organized chronologically. His numbering system is referred to with a J, then the number (for example, J651). The second scholar is R. W. Franklin, who published his collection a few decades after Johnson and reordered some poems based on new research. His numbering system is referred to with an F (for example, F1412). If the poem reference in a book or article has just a number, check the opening paragraph or introduction. The authors may have specified which scholar's order they are referencing there.

Another distinctive—and challenging—part of Dickinson's work is her use of punctuation. One of the first things most people learn about Dickinson is that she loved using dashes and frequently used them in place of more common punctuation marks like commas or periods. But she didn't just use horizontal dashes like the one in this sentence—she used vertical dashes, diagonal dashes, and dashes of drastically different lengths. Most publishers still have no practical way to represent all these different variations, so they will often choose to use either a hyphen or a medium-length dash in all instances. We have chosen to follow the source's usage in this book.

Dickinson also used irregular spellings and capitalization. Because her poems were handwritten (and frankly, her handwriting is a little messy), it is hard to tell which letters were capitalized and which were not. Even when it is clear what's a capital letter, many words are capitalized in the middle of lines that aren't proper nouns. Dickinson also used some unusual spellings, such as consistently spelling "yours" as "your's," or even spelling her name as both Emily and Emilie at various points in her life.

Finally, although many of Dickinson's poems use rhyme and meter, or poetic rhythm, in ways that are familiar, they also frequently break those rules. Dickinson was fond of a technique known as slant rhyme, or near rhyme, where words almost—but don't quite—rhyme. She was actually a bit of a pioneer in how frequently she used slant rhyme. Dickinson also liked to mix up her number of syllables per line so they didn't follow the established patterns that "good" poets were expected to use. Her meter will be explored in depth in chapter 2.

These quirks of Dickinson's writing can be a little challenging to adapt to at first, but they're also what make her poetry fun and interesting to read. They are why scholars continue to pore over scans of her manuscripts for details others have overlooked. And her creativity helped shake up our ideas of what poetry looks like, allowing future writers to try their own adventurous methods of poetry construction.

Edward Dickinson, like his father before him, was a firm believer in education for both boys and girls. Emily's father once wrote a series of articles for the Amherst newspaper outlining the proper roles that women and men should have in society. He believed that girls should be educated as well as boys, if they chose. However, he also believed that a woman had no place in business or politics but could best fulfill her role in life by having children and taking care of the home. In this way, Emily Norcross Dickinson was his ideal wife. But Edward's views on a woman's role would be challenged at every turn by his strong-willed eldest daughter.

Emily was an outgoing child, and she had many friends. One of her favorite playmates was Helen Fiske. Helen, Emily, and Emily's little sister, Vinnie, loved to hunt for berries and chestnuts. The girls spent a lot of time outdoors, and Emily developed a love and appreciation for nature. She spoke to the robins in the morning and to the orioles nesting in the cherry trees. Each spring Emily watched patiently for the daffodils to come up under the apple trees. She developed a special sense of the beauty of nature and of the relationship between nature and humans. Unlike children who found their joy in material things, Emily discovered her joy in the beauty and harmony of the natural world.

TWO

I AM GROWING HANDSOME VERY FAST INDEED

1840–1846

I n 1840, when Emily was nine years old, Edward
Dickinson left the other half of the Homestead that
they shared with the Mack family. He then moved
his wife and children to a larger house on West Street
(modern-day Pleasant Street). The Dickinsons would
make the white clapboard building their home for the next
sixteen years. The move left behind the debt and worries
of the old Homestead, giving the family a fresh start.

One benefit of the relocation was that Emily was
near Amherst Academy, the school her brother, Austin,
had attended. Fortunately, the school had been recently
opened to include girls. The academy allowed its female
students to sit in on classes with boys in subjects like
Latin as well as lectures for Amherst College. Such
access was rare in the period, especially for such a
small community as Amherst. Emily reveled in the
opportunities provided her at school. She studied,
among other subjects, grammar, composition, ancient
history, a wide variety of sciences (particularly geology),
logic, Latin, and math. The course of study at the
academy was intense, and it challenged Emily's mind.

Like most schools in nineteenth-century
Massachusetts, Amherst Academy was a religious
institution. Emily studied the Bible and attended
sermons and lectures on Christianity at the academy.
This, like Latin or geometry, would have been considered
a core part of her education. However, Emily and her
classmates had unusual leeway to express their opinions
and engage with their education. This was in no small
part because of their teachers. Many of the staff at
Amherst during the 1840s were young, charismatic new
graduates from Amherst College. They eagerly talked
with their students and treated pupils' ideas with respect.

Portrait of (*left to right*) Emily; her brother, Austin; and sister, Vinnie, in 1840

Emily enjoyed studying at the academy, and she made friends easily. Her friendships with four other girls were what made school the most fun. Abiah Root, Abby Wood, Harriet Merrill, Sarah Tracy, and Emily joined clubs like the Shakespeare Club and the Unseen Trap to read work aloud and exchange ideas. The girls wrote letters to one another, made up funny stories and jokes about their teachers, and shared confidences. They also went to parties together and wrote entertaining verses on Valentine's Day.

Emily made other friends, including Mattie and Sue Gilbert, Jane Humphrey, and Emily Fowler. Emily Fowler was the granddaughter of Noah Webster, the originator of the first dictionary and Samuel Fowler Dickinson's partner in founding Amherst College. Emily Fowler (later Ford) would become a writer in her own right, having her poetry and other writings published in numerous magazines, journals, and newspapers after she married. These friendships would continue through letters even after the girls left the academy.

Writing letters wasn't simply a means of keeping in touch. In the 1800s young people were expected to write letters early and often as a way to improve their grammar, spelling, and written expression. Letters were to be rewritten completely if they contained mistakes, and heaven help the writer who sent off correspondence with an inkblot. Emily took these instructions to heart, often writing drafts of her letters and then revising and polishing them before sending them off. She used letters to keep in touch with friends and family who weren't in Amherst and often pestered those who did not respond in kind. Her brother, Austin, became one of Emily's earliest and most frequent childhood correspondents.

Both Emily and Vinnie adored their older brother. When Austin left Amherst in the spring of 1842 to attend Williston Seminary, a boarding school in Easthampton, Massachusetts, Emily had difficulty adjusting to his absence. She found that writing to Austin shortened the distance between them.

Emily would remain particularly close with her brother, Austin, and would regularly write him letters until her death in 1886.

18 April 1842
My dear Brother
As Father was going to Northhampton and thought of coming over to see you I thought I would improve the opportunity and write you a few lines — We miss you very much indeed you cannot think how odd it seems without you there was always such a Hurrah wherever you was. . . . I *must now* close — all send a great deal of love to you and hope you are getting along well and — Enjoy your self —
Your affectionate Sister Emily —

Jane Humphrey lived with the Dickinson family while attending Amherst Academy and graduated a year before Emily. After Jane left Amherst, Emily began corresponding with her friend. In her letter, Emily expresses how much she and the other Dickinsons miss Jane. She also shares the latest school gossip and the details of everyday life.

DEAR READER:
LETTER-WRITING ETIQUETTE
IN THE 1800S

If not for her letters, Emily Dickinson would be even more of a mystery than she is. Her written record of her life is one of the most valuable resources scholars have to learn more about the enigmatic poet, and even then, she isn't always a reliable narrator. But did Dickinson's correspondents value her letters as much as people do today? In the 1800s, when letters were perhaps the most efficient and accessible ways to communicate with those near and far, it would be considered strange or downright rude not to write people. There were also strict guidelines about what and how to write which—shocker—Dickinson frequently broke.

The first rule of 1800s letter writing started before one word was written on the page. Letters could not be written on any old scratch paper. If letter writers wanted to be respected, they were supposed to use a full sheet (when possible) of heavier, more durable paper that would survive the sometimes rough journey through the mail. Writers were to avoid relying on printed or hand-drawn lines to keep their sentences straight and tidy. Letter etiquette was also starkly segregated by gender. Women were allowed to use lightly perfumed or colored paper, but men were forbidden from using anything but plain white stock. The ink used to write letters was to be simple black, both because it was easier to read and so it didn't fade with time and rereading. Self-sealing envelopes had been invented by the time Emily was writing letters, and that was much preferred to the old-fashioned method of sealing the letter at the folds with melted wax.

When it came to actually writing the letter, the rules depended on the type of person one was writing to and the letter writer's relationship to them. This had to be thought through at the outset, as even the way to address the recipient was governed by relationship. Young people courting through letters were expected to use a very limited set of topics and never be too casual, friendly, or gushing in their language. Lovers were judged as much for how closely they followed the rules of letter writing as for

Dickinson likely wrote this manuscript of a letter, to an unknown recipient, in early 1885.

what they wrote. For close friends, close relatives, and spouses, a wider variety of subjects was available, but again, language could not be sloppy or overly intimate. There was always a chance that someone else might receive or read a letter, so sharing secrets or private details via letter could have serious consequences.

Writers were advised to write in one of the "hands," or cursive handwriting styles of the day, such as English or Italian style. This lent formality to letters, as opposed to notes and lists that would be in one's typical handwriting. Finally, one was to close with a polite sign-off that again reflected their relationship to the recipient. They could also add a postscript from other people in their household (e.g., "Mother wishes you well") at the end of their formal letters, should they choose.

12 May 1842

My dear Jane

I have been looking for a letter from you this long time but not receiving any I plucked up all the remaining courage that I had left and determined to make one more effort to write to you a few lines — I want to see you very much for I have a great deal to tell you about school matters — and besides you are one of my dear friends. Sabra has had a beautiful ring given to her by Charles you know who as well as I do — the Examination at Easthampton is today — and Austin is coming home tonight. Father is sick with the Rheumatism and can not go but Mother has gone with somebody else — it is very unpleasant today — it showers most all the time. . . . I miss you more and more every day, in my study in play at home indeed every where I miss my beloved Jane — I wish you would write to me — I should think more of it than of a mine of gold — when you write me I wish you would write me a great long letter and tell me all the news that you know of — all your friends send a great deal of love to you . . . what good times we used to have jumping into bed when you slept with me. I do wish you would come to Amherst and make me a great long visit — how do you get along in Latin. I am in the class that you used to be in in Latin — besides Latin I study History and Botany I like the school very much indeed . . . answer this letter as soon as you can — I can think of nothing more to say now yours affectionately

Emily

The letter has the energy and scattershot attention of many eleven-year-olds, but it also contains early traces of Emily's trademark style. She spurns traditional punctuation for her trademark dashes and pours out her heart despite not receiving a reply to her letters. However, Jane was not the only friend with whom Emily became quickly and thoroughly attached.

Abiah Root only attended Amherst Academy for nine months, but she and Emily formed a fast friendship that would last a decade. In her earliest surviving letter to Abiah, Emily wrote:

23 February 1845

Dear Abiah,

After receiving the smitings of conscience for a long time, I have at length succeeded in stifling the voice of that faithful monitor by a promise of a long letter to you; so leave everything and sit down prepared for a long siege in the shape of a bundle of nonsense from friend E.

. . . I keep your lock of hair as precious as gold and a great deal more so. I often look at it when I go to my little lot of treasures, and wish the owner of that glossy lock were here. Old Time wags on pretty much as usual at Amherst, and I know of nothing that has occurred to break the silence; however, the reduction of the postage has excited my risibles somewhat. Only think! We can send a letter before long for five little coppers only, filled with the thoughts and advice of dear friends. But I will not get into a philosophizing strain just yet. There is time enough for that upon another page of this mammoth sheet. . . . Your *beau ideal* D. I have not seen lately. I presume he was changed into a star some night while gazing at them, and placed in the constellation Orion between Bellatrix and Betelgeux. I doubt not if he was here he would wish to be kindly remembered to you. . . .

I do wish you would come, 'Biah, and make me a long visit. If you will, I will entertain you to the best of my abilities, which you know are neither few nor small. Why can't you persuade your father and mother to let you come here to school next term, and keep me company, as I am going? Miss ———, I presume you can guess who I mean, is going to finish her education next summer. The finishing stroke is to be put on at [Norton]. She will then have learned all that we poor foot-travellers are toiling up the hill of knowledge to acquire. . . . We'll finish an education sometime, won't we? You may then be Plato, and I will be Socrates, provided you won't be wiser than I am. Lavinia just now interrupted my flow of thought by saying give my love to A. I presume you will be glad to have some one break off this epistle. All the girls send much love to you. And please accept a large share for yourself.

From your beloved.

Emily E. Dickinson.

[P.S.] . . . I hope this letter wont be broken open. If it is folks will wonder who has got so much nonsense to tell, wont they?

In the three years since her letters to Austin and Jane, Emily's letter-writing skills had considerably improved. At fourteen, she wrote smoothly and confidently, including references to ancient philosophers, astronomy, and fairy tales. Over the next several years, her letters to Abiah show her progression as a writer and her sense of humor and wit. A few months later, Emily wrote again to Abiah on school, family, and the trends of the day.

7 May 1845

Dear Abiah,

It seems almost an age since I have seen you, and it is indeed an age for friends to be separated. I was delighted to receive a paper from you, and I also was much pleased with the news it contained, especially that you are taking lessons on the "piny," as you always call it. But remember not to get on ahead of me. Father intends to have a piano very soon. How happy I shall be when I have one of my own! . . . Viny [Vinnie] went to Boston this morning with father, to be gone a fortnight, and I am left alone in all my glory. I suppose she has got there before this time, and is probably staring with mouth and eyes wide open at the wonders of the city. I have been to walk to-night, and got some very choice wild flowers. I wish you had some of them. . . . My plants look finely now. I am going to send you a little geranium leaf in this letter, which you must press for me. Have you made you an herbarium yet? I hope you will if you have not, it would be such a treasure to you; 'most all the girls are making one. If you do, perhaps I can make some additions to it from flowers growing around here. How do you enjoy your school this term? Are the teachers as pleasant as our old schoolteachers? I expect you have a great many prim, starched up young ladies there, who, I doubt not, are perfect models of propriety and good behavior. If they are, don't let your free spirit be chained by them. I don't know as there [are] any in school of this stamp. But there 'most always are a few, whom the teachers look up to and regard as their satellites. . . .

I had so many things to do for Viny, as she was going away, that very much against my wishes I deferred writing you until now, but forgive and forget, dear A., and I will promise to do better in future. Do write me soon, and let it be a long, long letter; and when you can't get time to write, send a paper, so as to let me know you think of me still, though we are separated by hill and stream. All the girls send much love to you. Don't forget to let me receive a letter from you soon. I can say no more now as my paper is all filled up.

Your affectionate friend,

Emily E. Dickinson

Like many writers, Emily was also a voracious reader. However, Edward Dickinson did not approve of reading, except books of a religious nature. He believed that "they joggle the Mind" and that other forms of education were more appropriate for a young woman to cultivate her skills as a future wife and mother. Edward Dickinson's views on reading were closely tied to the Calvinist community Emily grew up in.

But both Emily and Austin loved to read, and they often sneaked books into their rooms for what they called "reading feasts." Emily also encouraged her friends to read. She, along with other Amherst students, formed the Shakespeare Club. Emily, Austin, and their friends also traded books. Many of Emily's letters to friends include discussions of books they had read and exchanged with one another.

Emily was a sociable teenager. Besides the many girls and teachers with whom she grew close at school, she enjoyed spending time with the young men who worked at her father's office and with Austin's friends. Her mind was always open and inquiring, and she enjoyed discussing politics, business, and literature. Joseph Lyman, a schoolmate of Austin's and eventual friend of the family, was frequently surprised by her knowledge and wit.

In a letter to Abiah when she was fourteen, Emily joked that all the people in Amherst would soon be swooning over her, awaiting her beck and call.

> I am growing handsome very fast indeed! I expect I shall be the belle of Amherst when I reach my 17th year. I don't doubt that I shall have perfect crowds of admirers at that age. Then how I shall delight to make them await my bidding, and with what delight shall I witness their suspense while I make my final decision. But away with my nonsense.

Although her studies at the academy kept her very busy, Emily still had time for weekly piano and singing lessons. She became quite proficient at playing several tunes, such as "The Grave of Bonaparte" and "Maiden Weep No More," which were popular at the time. She also received her own piano during this time, which made it much easier for her to practice. Emily's appreciation for and ability to perform music would become a strength as she started writing poetry in earnest.

But her teenage years were not all music, friendship, and fun. Emily's bedroom window, which overlooked a graveyard, was a constant reminder of the grim facts of life and death. The mothers of three of Emily's schoolmates died in 1844. And in April of that year, when Emily was thirteen years old, her friend Sophia Holland died. The death was particularly difficult for Emily because she saw Sophia die—a traumatic event for anyone and especially for a girl losing a friend her age. Emily's sadness was so deep that her mother suggested she leave Amherst for a while. Emily decided to visit her Aunt Lavinia, who had moved to Boston.

Sophia's death made a lasting impression on Emily, and it took years for her to come to terms with it. It wasn't until two years later that she could write to Abiah about Sophia's death:

> My friend was Sophia Holland. She was too lovely for earth & she was transplanted from earth to heaven. I visited her often in sickness & watched over her bed. But at length Reason fled and the physician forbid any but the nurse to go into her room. Then it seemed to me I should die too if I could not be permitted to watch over her or even to look at her face. At length the doctor said she must die & allowed me to look at her a moment through the open door. I took off my shoes and stole softly to the sick room.
>
> There she lay mild & beautiful as in health & her pale features lit up with an unearthly — smile. I looked as long as friends would permit & when they told me I must look no longer I let them lead me away. I shed no tear, for my heart was too full to weep, but after she was laid in her coffin & I felt I could not call her back again I gave way to a fixed melancholy.

In September 1846, Emily returned to Boston to recover from an extended illness. It was the first time she had ever traveled alone, and despite the difficult circumstances, the trip offered new freedoms. Her aunt and two cousins, aware of Emily's grief over Sophia's death, attempted to lift her out of her melancholy. They felt that the best way to do this was to keep Emily busy, and Boston was the place to do this.

The sights were almost endless: Bunker Hill, museums, concerts, and botanical gardens, which were a special pleasure to Emily. She also visited Mount Auburn Cemetery and recounted its haunting beauty to Abiah. By the end of the month, Emily had somewhat recovered, although she still missed Sophia deeply.

HOLDING THEM CLOSE: HAIR LOCKS AND JEWELRY IN 1800S AMERICA

In the twenty-first century, hair is something to be cut, washed, styled, or removed. While many people enjoy and take pride in their hair and even see the cultural significance in different hairstyles and hair types, beyond the occasional baby book or scrapbook, keeping locks of hair is largely unheard of. Not so in 1800s New England.

In the nineteenth century, many women grew their hair out for their entire lives or only had it trimmed. The hair was cut from less visible sections so as to avoid ruining the highly stylized hairstyles of the day for both men and women. Fortunately for married women, they were expected to put their hair in elaborate updos after their wedding to show their movement into adulthood. These difficult styles made it easy to hide a shorter section of hair here and there. Men often slicked their hair back into polished, wet-looking styles that also made missing pieces easy to disguise. Girls and boys would just cut locks from the least visible bottom layer of their hair.

Hair was a placeholder for the person it was cut from. This tangible, but not improper, symbol of love was used between friends and lovers when they had to be apart, as some might never see each other again. School friends, especially girls, would trade locks of hair at the end of their term as a reminder of the friends they had made before they went their separate ways.

But there was a role for hair even more important than preserving friendships and romances: mourning. Victorian-era upper-class people had firm, detailed mourning rituals that had to be followed after a death. This included dressing in all black for at least a year, then gradually transitioning back to wearing normal clothes. It also included public displays of grief and receiving support from family and friends. Mourning was a household duty like cooking and cleaning, and like most domestic work, it fell to women.

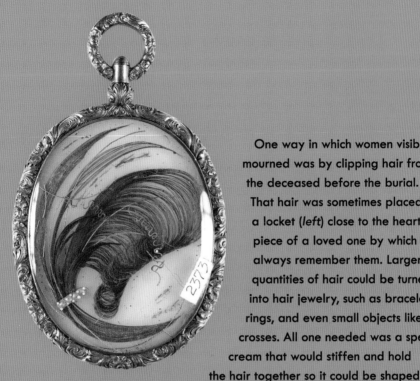

One way in which women visibly mourned was by clipping hair from the deceased before the burial. That hair was sometimes placed in a locket (*left*) close to the heart—a piece of a loved one by which to always remember them. Larger quantities of hair could be turned into hair jewelry, such as bracelets, rings, and even small objects like crosses. All one needed was a special cream that would stiffen and hold the hair together so it could be shaped and molded. This practice was so popular that women's magazines of the 1800s included patterns and ideas for hair jewelry that women could try. They formed crafting circles to work with hair, which also served as a grief support group for the woman or women who had lost a loved one.

As the Civil War thrust death into the lives of almost every family in America, mourning rituals changed. Even more value was placed on remembering and honoring the dead, and practices such as hairweaving took on an even greater significance. Other practices such as death photography, where a corpse was posed and photographed shortly after death, became common. These efforts contained death to an established ritual that mourners could go through to help cope with loss and move on. In a society wracked by death, one could not dwell too long on those lost and lose sight of those that remained.

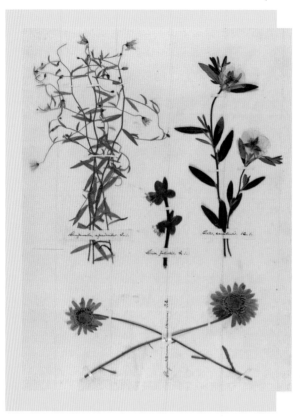

Emily's herbarium included more than four hundred specimens.

During this period, Emily also decided to undertake a new project: a botanical book. Emily had studied plants and flowers at the academy. She had also been newly encouraged by the botanical exhibitions and lectures she had attended in Boston. Emily spent weeks afterward exploring the woods near her home.

Primroses and heliotrope, jasmine and gillyflowers, mignonette and sweet alyssum—they were all gathered gently into Emily's apron and brought home. She spent hours drying the flowers and mounting them into a bound book. Emily carefully wrote the name of each flower, first in Latin and then in English. By the time she had completed her project, more than four hundred different varieties of flowers were exhibited in her book, her herbarium. Her scientific knowledge of plants and her attachment to their beauty informed her poems in the coming years. In several pieces, Emily's poems wove together her love of nature and her deepest feelings.

"Nature" is what We see -
The Hill - the Afternoon -
Squirrel - Eclipse - the Bumble bee -
Nay - Nature is Heaven -

"Nature" is what We hear -
The Bobolink - the Sea -
Thunder - the Cricket -
Nay - Nature is Harmony -

"Nature" is what We know -
But have no Art to say -
So impotent our Wisdom is
To Her Sincerity -

Emily often related nature to other things she was familiar with, weaving together different spheres to create wholly unexpected images. She also connected nature to her moods, particularly in reference to the seasons, and marveled at creatures large and small. However, she also defied traditional nature poetry of the time by exploring the darker and more challenging elements of the natural world.

WHISTLE WHILE YOU WORK: MUSIC IN EMILY DICKINSON'S POETRY

Emily Dickinson studied music from an early age. Her aunt Lavinia referred to Dickinson discovering "the moosic" when the girl was just a toddler, and she never lost her fascination with it. After taking piano and singing lessons through her teens, the poet was a confident performer who sometimes showed off her talents by composing haunting melodies on the spot on her piano, often playing in the dead of night. And as part of the community of Amherst, Dickinson was exposed to countless hymns when she went to church with her family.

All the musical elements of Dickinson's childhood coalesced in adulthood into a strong understanding of rhyme, meter, and the power of performance. When the poet started seriously writing in the 1850s, she began by strictly following the familiar beats of the hymns of her youth. In the poem "It's all I have to bring today," Dickinson perfectly adheres to the common meter. It consists of repeating patterns of eight beats per line and six beats per line. Split into syllables, the opening lines read,

> It's / all / I / have / to / bring / to- / day -
> This, / and / my / heart / be- / side -
> This, / and / my / heart, / and / all / the / fields -
> And / all / the / mead- / ows / wide -

Many hymns that utilized the common meter followed an alternating *abab* rhyme scheme, but Dickinson often disregarded such strict rhyming conventions. This poem rhymes the second and fourth lines, side and wide, as well as the sixth and eighth lines, tell and dwell. The rhyme scheme would then be written as *abcb, defe*, with each new letter representing a different ending sound such as "ide" or "ell."

Other metric patterns that Dickinson used exactly or slightly altered are the long meter (eight beats in each line) and the short meter (six beats, six beats, eight beats, six beats). Dickinson frequently organized her stanzas, or poetic sections, as quatrains that contain four lines each.

Dickinson played and composed music on this piano in the Homestead. It remains in the Emily Dickinson Museum in Amherst, below portraits of Dickinson's parents.

Beyond traditional hymn meters and rhymes, Dickinson also set her poetry to the rhythms of specific songs. For instance, many of her poems can be set to the 1850s song "The Yellow Rose of Texas." While the song was hailed as one of America's great Western folk songs in the twentieth century, the original lyrics come from a blackface minstrel show in 1853. A decade later, the song was used as a rallying cry for Texas Confederate troops. Despite these associations, the song was incredibly popular in the 1850s and '60s and—after its revisions—from the 1930s through the 1980s in various forms.

While "The Yellow Rose of Texas" was around during Dickinson's lifetime, it is far from the only song that fits Dickinson's verses. In fact, the rhythms Dickinson uses are still popular, and one can set several of her shorter works to the theme song from *Gilligan's Island* or other modern tunes.

THREE

I CARED LESS FOR RELIGION THAN EVER

1847–1849

One day, sixteen-year-old Emily wrote to her friend Abiah about religious revival meetings that had taken place in Amherst a few days before:

> The meetings were thronged by people old and young. . . . It was really wonderful to see how near heaven came to sinful mortals. Many who felt there was nothing in religion determined to go once & see if there was anything in it, and they were melted at once. . . . I attended none of the meetings last winter. I felt that I was so easily excited that I might again be deceived and I dared not trust myself.

In the 1830s, New England was at the tail end of the Second Great Awakening, a religious movement designed to revive lost faith and recruit new members into local churches. The sweeping changes carried into the mid-1800s, reaching Amherst in the 1840s and '50s. But the movement did more than bring back ideas of organized religion lost after the Revolutionary War. The Second Great Awakening brought with it a change in attitude toward Christianity and faith that would shape Emily Dickinson and her contemporaries' approach to their faith.

One of the ways preachers convinced new members to join their congregation was by throwing revival meetings. These special sermons and outdoor events were focused entirely on stirring up religious fervor, often with vivid and, at times, horrifying imagery of the fates that awaited nonbelievers. Everyone was a sinner, the preachers loudly proclaimed, and unless people confessed their sins and took refuge in God, they would suffer the fires of damnation. Audience members were encouraged to make public declarations that they were ready to accept God and be saved from this fate.

The threat of eternal damnation was not taken lightly by God-fearing people. Death at a young age was a frequent occurrence in the 1800s. Diseases such as pneumonia, tuberculosis, scarlet fever, and smallpox were common. Drinking water was often contaminated, and death from cholera and typhoid was not unusual. The complications from a simple cold could result in death. For those who survived their youth, the average adult life span was still only fifty-five. Most sermons preached that dying without accepting God was a path to endless torture in hell. With constant reminders that death could happen at any time, people felt a strong pressure to join and stay within the church. Even faithful believers wanted to be reassured that their life after death would be better than their life on Earth.

Life in Amherst in the 1800s centered around religion. Emily's mother and many others like her believed in a judgmental God who meted out punishment if people didn't do things to make him happy. She believed that if misfortune befell herself or her family, it was because God was showing his displeasure. Her father was also a devout member of the church. He read the Bible each night to his family, and he wanted to be thought of as a God-fearing man in his community.

Emily expressed a skepticism about parts of her religious community early in her teens. By the time Emily was sixteen years old, she had begun to discard the religion of her community and parents. She stopped regularly attending church services and revival meetings, partly because she could not square the vengeful, wrathful God of the Old Testament to the love and peace advocated by Christ in the New Testament. She also eschewed the idea that the only path to God was through church attendance and organized Bible study. Emily saw elements of the divine in everything, especially in nature, as evidenced in the following poem:

Outdoor church services known as camp meetings were popular during the Second Great Awakening. People from miles away would gather at a previously arranged location to camp and attend services for several days. Curiosity, social opportunities, and religious fervor were all motivators for attendants.

The Bumble of a Bee -
A Witchcraft, yieldeth me.
If any ask me "Why" -
'Twere easier to die
Than tell!

The Red opon the Hill
Taketh away my will -
If anybody sneer,
Take care - for God is near -
That's all!

The Breaking of the Day -
Addeth to my Degree -
If any ask me "how" -
Artist who drew me so -
Must tell!

One by one, Emily's friends were converted, but she resisted. She wrote to Abiah: "I soon forgot my morning prayer or else it was irksome to me. One by one my old habits returned and I cared less for religion than ever."

Emily took a firm stand with her family. She patiently listened to the Bible readings and attended an occasional church service with her parents. But she refused to get involved in the religious activities of the community.

In 1847, Emily enrolled in the Mount Holyoke Female Seminary in South Hadley, Massachusetts, along with about three hundred other young women, There were three grades—junior, middle, and senior. Sixteen-year-old Emily entered as a junior, but before the year was out she would be taking classes in the senior division.

Emily was homesick. She was only a few miles from Amherst, but she missed her family and friends. She also missed engaging in discussions at home and school, where she was treated as an intellectual equal by those years older than herself. In Amherst, Emily had access to all sorts of books, newspapers, and educated visitors with whom she could discuss politics and current events. But education at Mount Holyoke would prove much different than at Amherst Academy.

While away in South Hadley, Emily struggled to adjust to the secluded, highly religious atmosphere of the college. She wrote to Austin with humor and sarcasm about her frustrations—especially feeling separate from life outside of Mount Holyoke.

South Hadley, 21 October 1847
My dear Brother. Austin.
. . . Won't you please tell me when you answer my letter

ART FROM LOSS: DICKINSON'S POETRY ON DEATH

For those with only casual knowledge of Emily Dickinson, the one thing they likely know is she wrote about death—a lot. Dozens of Dickinson's poems fixate on death and dying, and countless more mention it or use it as a metaphor. Given Dickinson's early and frequent exposure to death and the period in which she lived, such a fascination makes sense. However, the poet went beyond the typical boundaries and ideas on death into territory that was solely her own.

In poems like "I Felt a Funeral, in my Brain," Dickinson uses the familiar events of a funeral to describe her own inner torment. The speaker describes mourners "treading - treading" across her brain in heavy steps with an unrelenting rhythm. The coffin lid shuts, the mourners leave, and the speaker remains in despair, searching for answers. Finally, "a Plank in Reason, broke, / And I dropped down, and down" into unknown, unexplored worlds. The speaker has given in to the madness.

Another poem, "Dying! To be afraid of thee," explores the pain of those left behind to mourn. The speaker explains that one needs only fear death if they "Have left exposed a Friend" to death. If one has no friends who the candidate for President is? I have been trying to find out ever since I came here & have not yet succeeded. I don't know anything more about affairs in the world, than if I was in a trance, & you must imagine with all your "Sophomoric discernment," that it is but little & very faint. Has the Mexican war terminated yet & how? Are we beat? Do you know of any nation about to besiege South Hadley? If so, do inform me of it, for I would be glad of a chance to escape, if we are to be stormed. I suppose Miss Lyon. would furnish us all with daggers & order us to fight for our lives, in case such perils should befall us. . . .

Your aff. Emily

in danger, one has nothing to fear. Dickinson uses the imagery of war in the poem as well: armies, artillery, enemies, and batteries, or groups of soldiers and weapons. The poem, dated to 1864, during the height of the Civil War, unites a soldier and a civilian's shared struggle with death surrounding them. It could also reflect that Dickinson's closest "friends" almost all escaped the war unharmed.

Dickinson also used the topic of death to explore her complicated relationship to faith. While some of her letters indicate the poet believed in a version of heaven, she also expressed doubts. In "I never felt at Home – Below" the speaker explains he will not feel at home in heaven, just as he does not on Earth. Nothing changes in heaven, creating a boring, constant world with no change. Instead, he invited God to visit or just nap "So not to see us," instead of always watching. The poem concludes with the admission that one cannot escape death and God, as someday, Judgment Day will arrive.

Like all of her poetry, Dickinson's ruminations on death are open to numerous interpretations and are continually reevaluated. They offer rich insight into the poet's psyche and how she processed the trauma and grief of her life, channeling it into her art.

Mount Holyoke

Another major change for Emily was the strict schedule of Mount Holyoke. Nearly every minute of her day was planned out—a far cry from her days spent wandering her family's land and meeting up with friends. There were also more than seventy rules that students had to follow. By early November, Emily had adjusted some to her new surroundings and felt less homesick. She wrote to her friend Abiah, giving her a picture of the Mount Holyoke school year and schedule:

> South Hadley, 6 November 1847
>
> My Dear Abiah.
>
> I am really at Mt. Holyoke Seminary & this is to by my home for a long year. Your affectionate letter was joyfully received & I wish that this might make you as happy as your's did me. It has been nearly six weeks since I left home & that is a longer time, than I was ever away from home before now. I was very homesick for a few days & it seemed to me I could not live here. But I am now contented & quite happy, if I can be happy when absent from my dear home & friends . . . you must remember that I have a very dear home & that this is my first trial in the way of absence for any length of time in my life. As you desire it, I will give you a full account of myself since I first left the paternal roof. . . .

The school is very large & though quite a number have left, on account of finding the examinations more difficult than they anticipated, yet there are nearly 300. now. Perhaps you know that Miss. Lyon is raising her standard of scholarship a good deal, on account of the number of applicants this year & on account of that she makes the examinations more severe than usual. . . .

I room with my Cousin Emily, who is a Senior. She is an excellent room-mate & does all in her power to make me happy. You can imagine how pleasant a good room-mate is, for you have been away to school so much. Everything is pleasant & happy here & I think I could be no happier at any other school away from home. Things seem much more like home than I anticipated & the teachers are all very kind & affectionate to us. They call on us frequently & urge us to return their calls & when we do, we always receive a cordial welcome from them.

I will tell you my order of time for the day, as you were so kind as to give me your's. At 6. oclock, we all rise. We breakfast at 7. Our study hours begin at 8. At 9. we all meet in Seminary Hall, for devotions. At 10¼. I recite a review of Ancient History, in connection with which we read Goldsmith & Grimshaw [authors of History texts]. At .11. I recite a lesson in "Pope's Essay on Man" which is merely transposition. At .12. I practice Calisthenics & at 12¼ read until dinner, which is at 12½ & after dinner, from 1½ until 2 I sing in Seminary Hall. From 2¾ until 3¾. I practise upon the Piano. At 3¾ I go to Sections, where we give in all our accounts for the day, including, Absence – Tardiness – Communications – Breaking Silent Study hours – Receiving Company in our rooms & ten thousand other things, which I will not take time or place to mention. At 4½. we go into Seminary Hall, & receive advice from Miss. Lyon in the form of a lecture. We have Supper at 6. & silent-study hours from then until the retiring bell, which rings at 8¾, but the tardy bell does not ring until 9¾, so that we dont often obey the first warning to retire.

Unless we have a good & reasonable excuse for failure upon any of the items, that I mentioned above, they are recorded & a *black mark* stands against our names: As you can easily imagine, we do not like very well to get "exceptions" as they are called scientifically here. My domestic work is not difficult & consists in carrying the Knives from the 1st tier of tables at morning & noon & at night washing & wiping the same quantity of Knives. I am quite well & hope to be able to spend the year here, free from sickness. . . .

Abiah, you must write me often & I shall write you as often as I have time. But you know I have many letters to write now I am away from home. Cousin. Emily says "Give my love to Abiah."

From your aff

Emily E. D—

In addition to the academic schedule, two thirty-minute periods were allotted each day for meditation and prayer, which suited Emily quite well. She enjoyed her quiet time alone, away from the noise and bustle of the rest of the day. She even chose to skip optional school events like seeing an animal menagerie that visited the campus in favor of getting more time to herself, remarking "I enjoyed the solitude finely."

Mount Holyoke Seminary was run by a young scholar and devout Christian, Mary Lyon. Mary Lyon was determined to save the souls of each of the young students that passed through the halls of her school. She had founded the seminary as a means to not only convert students but to enlist their help in spreading faith and converting others far beyond South Hadley.

There were three levels of education at Mount Holyoke, but there were also three religious classifications. They were "Christians," "Hopers," and "No-Hopers." As the name implies, Christians were girls who had already confessed their faith and joined the church. Hopers were students who believed they were close to converting to Christianity, and No-Hopers were those who had no intention of joining the church.

Although a good number of Mount Holyoke's 230 students (after about 70 students failed to pass their exams and left) were Christians, there were dozens who fell into the Hoper and No-Hoper categories. The latter two groups were frequently singled out for extra meetings and prayer events with Miss Lyon and the other teachers on staff in the hopes of pushing them to accept Christ.

Miss Lyon instilled in her young women the principles of discipline, honesty, and a strong self-will, in addition to firm Christian beliefs. She was dedicated to giving her students the best education she could. One of her favorite expressions was "We have great power over ourselves. We may become almost what we will."

EMILY DICKINSON'S SCHEDULE AT MOUNT HOLYOKE

6:00 a.m.	Rise for the day
7:00 a.m.	Breakfast
8:00 a.m.	Study hours begin
9:00 a.m.	Devotions in Seminary Hall
10:15 a.m.	History class
11:00 a.m.	Recite poem on ethics, from memory
12:00 p.m.	Calisthenics
12:15 p.m.	Reading (free time)
12:30 p.m.	Dinner (lunch)
1:30 p.m.	Singing practice in Seminary Hall
2:45 p.m.	Piano practice
3:45 p.m.	Daily reports
4:30 p.m.	Lecture from Miss Lyon
6:00 p.m.	Supper
After supper	Silent study hours
8:45 p.m.	First bell for lights out
9:45 p.m.	Second bell for lights out

WILL YOU BE MINE:
VALENTINE'S DAY VERSE
IN 1800s AMHERST

Celebrations of Saint Valentine were part of American culture long before the rise of giant stuffed bears and candy hearts. As Puritanism loosened its grip on New England society, more and more people accepted the idea of marrying for love (or at least the appearance of it) rather than for family through arranged marriages. This new focus led to a rise in courtship rituals that allowed young people to show their interest in each other.

One popular way of expressing affection was through highly stylized love poetry, and Valentine's Day became a popular occasion for doing so. Hopeful lovers could either try their hand at writing their own verse to show off their creativity and skill or use a classic love poem that their recipient would be familiar with. This decision was not to be taken lightly, as some exchanges begun on Valentine's Day could lead to formal courtship and eventually marriage.

Exchanging valentine verses was not just for lovers, though. Friends often exchanged poems and notes as well, either satirizing the conventions of love poetry or just practicing for their later exchanges. Emily Dickinson seems to have reveled in writing valentine works, as some of her very first archived writings are of valentines sent to friends.

In addition to the poem itself, writers could convey all sorts of hidden messages through the paper they used, how text was arranged, and what, if anything, was included with the valentine verse. These decisions could feel overwhelming and time-consuming. Fortunately, a major solution was about to be introduced.

In 1849 an enterprising student at Mount Holyoke named Esther Howland asked her brother to bring her back one of the wildly popular Valentine's Day verse cards from his trip to England. He did, and she immediately saw the potential to bring the creation to the American market. The daughter of a stationery creator (known as stationers) with access to cheap labor from her fellow college students, Esther had all the resources she needed. She recruited girls from Mount Holyoke and formed what some claim was the real first assembly-line process in the United States.

Girls at her makeshift dorm workshop took pretty, embossed paper made by Esther's father and painstakingly added paper flowers, cutouts, imported fabrics, and a range of valentine verses Esther curated herself. Esther also added a stylized *H* to the back of each of her cards to mark it as an official Howland product—a forward-thinking move that would serve her well in the coming years. By the mid-1850s, Esther and her copycats' cards were so successful and ubiquitous that a *New York Times* article declared them useless and impersonal.

By her thirties, Esther had a booming business with a factory that distributed cards across New England and fetched prices as high as fifty dollars—the cost of a horse and buggy! She continued building her empire after an accident made her a wheelchair user and only sold her company in 1880 so she could care for her dying father. Despite founder Mary Lyon's best intentions, valentines would play a role in the lives of two of Mount Holyoke's early famous graduates.

Miss Lyon constantly reinforced her beliefs both through her teachings and through her kindnesses to all of her students. She made sure that the other teachers did likewise. Emily once commented on this in a letter to Abiah: "One thing is certain & that is, that Miss. Lyon & all the teachers, seem to consult our comfort & happiness in everything they do & you know that is pleasant."

The students at Mount Holyoke were allowed to go home for Thanksgiving. Emily's brother and father came to pick her up from school, and she noted the tears in her mother's eyes as she came in the door. She had a great time while she was at home for the holiday, and she missed the warmth and coziness of her home more than ever when she returned to school. After seeing friends and family at Thanksgiving, she didn't want to leave home ever again.

Emily returned to her arduous schedule, however, and continued to excel in her studies. But by the time Christmas came, she was once again terribly homesick. And Christmas being considered at the time more of a pagan ritual than a family holiday, students were not allowed to go home. On Christmas Eve, Miss Lyon announced that Christmas Day would be celebrated with fasting and prayer. That meant that the girls were not allowed out of their rooms for the day. They were to go without meals, and they were to spend the time praying.

After making her pronouncement to the assembly of young women, Miss Lyon asked all to stand as an acknowledgment of their commitment to the spiritual agenda that she had just mapped out for them. Every student attending stood up—except Emily. Her quiet defiance didn't earn her a punishment, surprisingly, but her behavior made her seem strange in the eyes of her believer peers.

In February 1848, Miss Lyon lectured the girls on the foolishness of valentine cards. She told them that sending valentines was expressly forbidden and anyone caught doing so would be severely reprimanded. Again, Emily decided that Miss Lyon was not going to dictate to her. She enlisted the aid of the postmaster at South Hadley. More than 150 valentine cards went out from Mount Holyoke, all of them sent by Emily.

In March 1848, Emily developed a hacking cough. Because a severe cough could lead to pneumonia and death, Edward Dickinson decided that Emily would heal faster at home under her mother's care. A month later, when Emily was recovering, she continued her studies at home.

Her recovery was an opportunity for her to read books and poems other than those required by the school. Austin gave his sister a copy of Henry Wadsworth Longfellow's romantic novel, *Kavanagh*. He became one of Emily's favorite poets, as did Elizabeth Barrett Browning. Emily also read the novels of Charlotte and Emily Brontë.

As Emily's health improved, she spent time with her friends going for walks in the woods. They were amazed at her familiarity with the wild plants that grew there. Emily was a social, well-liked girl in her hometown. After returning to school, Emily wrote to Abiah of her experiences while at home in Amherst:

> South Hadley, 16 May 1848
> My dear Abiah,
> . . . The older I grow, the more do I love spring and spring flowers. Is it so with you? While at home there were several pleasure parties of which I was a member, and in our rambles we found many and beautiful children of spring, which I will mention and see if you have found them, — the trailing arbutus, adder's tongue, yellow violets, liver-leaf, blood-root, and many other smaller flowers.
> What are you reading now? I have little time to read when I am here, but while at home I had a feast in the reading line, I can assure you. Two or three of them I will mention: *Evangeline* [a poem by Henry Wadsworth Longfellow]. *The Princess* [by Alfred, Lord Tennyson], *The Maiden Aunt* [by Marcelle Bute Smedley], *The Epicurean* [by Thomas Moore], and *The Twins and Heart* by Tupper, complete the list. Am I not a pedant for telling you what I have been reading? . . .
> Ever your own affectionate
> Emilie E. Dickinson.

A CHANGING LEGACY:
QUEERNESS AT MOUNT HOLYOKE

When Emily Dickinson attended Mount Holyoke Seminary, the college was committed to educating a new generation of religious leaders. The college was the first in an organization known as the Seven Sisters. The Seven Sisters was a kind of Ivy League for women's colleges. These institutions brought higher learning to women across New England, at a time when educating women beyond secondary school was seen as a waste of time.

At the start of the twentieth century, Mount Holyoke began another legacy as a school addressing queer issues. In 1901, Mary Woolley took over as president of Mount Holyoke and transitioned the college toward being a conventional but respected institution for higher education. Woolley would not go through the challenge alone. Jeannette Marks, a student of Woolley's while she was a professor at Wellesley College, would join the faculty of Mount Holyoke as an English professor shortly after Woolley's appointment. The pair were life partners for fifty years, living together until her death in 1947.

Woolley and Marks were not subtle about their relationship. According to an exhibit by Mount Holyoke students, "Woolley's habit of scaling three flights of stairs each night to kiss Marks goodnight did not go unnoticed by the student population, who viewed it as alternately amusing or embarrassing." Despite the unusual nature of their relationship for the early 1900s, both women were respected by the staff and students. This openness was a sign of the boldness of future generations of queer women at Mount Holyoke.

In the 1960s and '70s, visibility and activism by and for queer people was scarce. But at the small liberal arts college, lesbian and bisexual culture thrived. The Lesbian Bisexual Alliance (LBA) was formed in 1979 as a way for queer women to support and network with each other. Although the group got pushback from heterosexual students in the 1980s who felt "scared to death" of talking about being straight, they remained a strong presence at the school. In 2014 Mount Holyoke became the second all-women's college in the United States to admit transgender students. If Emily had attended the college a century later, she would have been among those women pushing at the limits of acceptability in art and identity.

Edward Dickinson decided Emily would not continue her schooling after the spring term was over. Emily had mixed feelings after hearing that this would be her final semester at Mount Holyoke. On the one hand, she was happy to be going home. There was a part of her, however, that regretted not being able to continue her formal education. She also regretted that she had not succumbed to becoming a formal Christian, as most of her friends had. She wrote to Abiah:

Father has decided not to send me to Holyoke another year, so this is my *last term*. . . . It startles me when I really think of the advantages I have had, and I fear I have not improved them as I ought. . . . I regret that last term, when that golden opportunity was mine, that I did not give up and become a Christian. It is not now too late, so my friends tell me, so my offended conscience whispers, but it is hard for me to give up the world.

In August 1848, Emily left Mount Holyoke for good. Seven months later, in March 1849, Mary Lyon died. Emily read the obituary notice in the newspapers. Many years later, Emily would write the following poem. Perhaps she was thinking of Mary Lyon when she wrote it.

I went to thank Her -
But She Slept -
Her Bed - a funneled Stone -
With Nosegays at the Head and Foot -
That Travellers - had thrown -

Who went to thank Her -
But She Slept -
'Twas Short - to cross the Sea -
To look opon Her like - alive -
But turning back - 'twas slow -

FOUR

MY LIFE WAS MADE A VICTIM

1850–1854

The year 1850 brought drastic changes to both Amherst and the nation. Millard Fillmore was sworn in as the United States' thirteenth president after the death of Zachary Taylor. California entered the Union as a free state, and the Fugitive Slave Act was passed as part of the Compromise of 1850, which delayed the Civil War for a decade. And in Massachusetts, yet another revival was sweeping through towns and cities, converting Austin and Edward Dickinson and leaving Emily as the sole nonbeliever of the family. Emily learned of these and other issues of her day through a variety of local and national newspapers and magazines.

No fewer than fifteen different publications were delivered monthly to the Dickinson home. Publications such as the *Observer*, *New England Farmer*, and the *Boston Courier* were read by all members of Emily's family. With four newspapers, three religious magazines, three literary magazines, and two publications dealing with law and politics, the Dickinson household was kept well informed about the important developments of their day.

Emily also had access to an excellent collection of books. Edward Dickinson's library was filled with books of poetry and classics carefully selected to reflect those that he considered fit reading for everyone in his household. Emily chose to read the novels of Charles Dickens; the poems of Alfred, Lord Tennyson; and Henry Wadsworth Longfellow; and the essays of philosopher and writer Ralph Waldo Emerson.

However, Edward's library was not Emily's only source of reading material. Charlotte Brontë was Emily's favorite author. Brontë's novel *Jane Eyre*, published

A steady stream of publications through the Dickinson household meant that Emily was never without new reading material.

under a pseudonym in 1847, was becoming popular. It was not the type of book that Edward Dickinson would have had in his library. He would have felt that the heroine's free and independent lifestyle would give Emily ideas. But a young clerk in her father's law office had read the book and told Emily about it. She asked to borrow it and probably read it without her father's knowledge.

She kept the book for three months and read it several times. She loaned it to Sue Gilbert, and they spent hours discussing the book.

Emily felt a bond with the heroine of the book, Jane Eyre. The connection made sense, as in some ways, she and Jane were similar. Emily was close to Jane in age—Jane was eighteen and Emily nineteen. Emily shared some of Jane's physical characteristics—she had a small build and a plain face. In the book, Jane wanted to look different than she did, to be prettier, taller—qualities Emily herself wished for. And Jane Eyre was high-spirited and adventurous—qualities used by friends and family to describe Emily in her teens and early twenties.

Emily differed from Jane, however, in the way she lived her life. While Jane lived a life consistent with an adventurous nature, Emily lived quietly in Amherst, rarely venturing forth from the little town. Reading about Jane Eyre may have made Emily long for a more independent lifestyle, one in which she was free to come and go as she pleased.

At nineteen, Emily was old enough to be married and have children, yet she was still treated as a child by her father. Her brother moved to Boston to teach, but whenever Emily tried to become more independent, she was reprimanded for it. Edward seemed to have no intention of letting his eldest daughter set out on her own. Emily also felt the weight of caring for her mother, who continued to suffer ill health and bouts of depression when her husband was away.

In May 1850, Emily wrote to Abiah about her frustration. When she wanted to go riding with a friend, she felt she couldn't leave her mother and her duties.

> 7 and 17 May 1850
>
> Dear Remembered.
>
> . . . When I am not at work in the kitchen, I sit by the side of mother, provide for her little wants — and try to cheer, and encourage her. I ought to be glad, and grateful that I *can* do anything now, but I do feel so very lonely, and so anxious to have her cured. I hav'nt repined but *once*, and you shall know all the why. While I washed dishes at noon in that little "sink-room" of our's, I heard a well-known rap, and a friend I love *so* dearly came and asked me to ride in the woods, the sweet-still woods, and I wanted to exceedingly — I told him I could not go, and he said he was disappointed — he wanted me very much — then the tears came into my eyes, tho' I tried to choke them back, and he said I *could*, and *should* go, and it seemed to me unjust. Oh I struggled with great temptation, and it cost me much of denial, but I think in the end I conquered . . .
>
> I went cheerfully round my work, humming a little air till mother had gone to sleep, then cried with all my might, seemed to think I was much abused, that this wicked world was unworthy such devoted, and terrible sufferings, and came to my various senses in great dudgeon at life, and time, and love for affliction, and anguish. . . .
>
> Your aff friend,
> Emily.

JANE EYRE.

An Autobiography.

EDITED BY
CURRER BELL

IN THREE VOLUMES.
VOL. I.

LONDON:
SMITH, ELDER, AND CO., CORNHILL.
1847.

Jane Eyre is considered a revolutionary novel for its portrayal of the titular character's moral and spiritual development through a first-person narrative. The book explores topics of class, religion, and feminism.

READING INTO IT:
POPULAR NOVELS AND STORIES OF
THE MID-NINETEENTH CENTURY

One way to understand a writer's style is to read what they have read. Like most poets and authors, Emily Dickinson was a voracious reader who enjoyed not just the highbrow "literary" works of her day but also popular poetry, short stories, and novels that her schoolmates and friends would have been familiar with. Some of these writings included novels *Kavanagh* and *Jane Eyre*, the serial story (and later novel) *David Copperfield*, and the poetry of Elizabeth Barrett Browning, John Keats, and Ralph Waldo Emerson. There were also countless other works Emily would have read in the newspapers and journals she received at home and books she may have felt were too common or salacious to describe reading in her letters.

The novel *Kavanagh* by Henry Wadsworth Longfellow follows the intersecting lives of people in a small New England village. Preacher Mr. Kavanagh moves to the town and starts spreading his gentle message of Christianity to the townspeople. Schoolmaster Mr. Churchill tries to help the new pastor settle in while telling all his friends and neighbors about the great romance novel he will someday write, if he ever gets around to starting it. Meanwhile, best friends Cecilia and Alice grow closer and closer to each other, with their passion bordering on romantic, which confuses them both. However, after encountering Mr. Kavanagh, who has been chosen as the town's new pastor, both girls fall in love with him, and their friendship frays. Kavanagh and Cecilia marry, Alice dies in despair, and Mr. Churchill never quite gets around to starting his book. Although the novel is largely unknown today and is not considered Longfellow's greatest work by any means, writers including Ralph Waldo Emerson, Nathaniel Hawthorne, and of course Emily Dickinson read and appreciated it. For Emily, it could be that the novel's rural New England setting, homoerotic friendships, and examination of what it means to be a writer struck a chord.

Charlotte Brontë's famous novel *Jane Eyre* is the story of the titular heroine as she tries to survive as an orphan and governess. After losing her parents at a young age and growing up with her barely tolerant aunt and cousins, Jane escapes to Lowood Institution. However, the charity school for orphans is even worse, and the conditions keep the girls on the brink of starvation and disease. After the old headmaster dies, conditions improve and Jane is able to prove herself as a student and a teacher at the school before moving on to a governess position at Thornfield Hall. There she meets Edward Rochester, her boss and the former lover of the girl she is teaching, who keeps a terrible secret. His wife, Bertha Mason, is locked in the third floor of the Thornfield manor due to her apparent insanity. Jane falls in love with Rochester, but she runs away after learning of his wife and ends up at a clergyman's home. She discovers the clergyman and his sisters are actually her cousins, and she has family after all. However, the clergyman tries to force Jane to marry him and move to India, at which point she runs back to Thornfield to find it burned to the ground, Bertha dead, and Rochester partly blinded. This frees Rochester to marry Jane, and the two wed and have a son and a happy life together. This densely packed, psychologically thrilling novel gave power to women's perspectives and the many hardships they experience, as well as exploring complicated ideas of sanity and fidelity.

David Copperfield, one of Charles Dickens's novels published chapter by chapter in magazines, told the full life story of the titular character. David's life starts out rather well, albeit with his father passing away early, but after David's mother marries the cruel Mr. Murdstone and David fights his abusive stepfather, he is shipped off to boarding school where he is again beaten regularly. But after David is orphaned, Mr. Murdstone sends his ten-year-old stepson to work at a bottling factory and live with the impoverished Micawber family until Mr. Micawber is sent to debtor's prison. David runs away to his eccentric great-aunt Betsey Trotwood's home, and she helps him reenter school and stay with a local family with a daughter named Agnes. The two children become fast friends. David matures, starts work as a secretary and a writer, and unwittingly gets involved in the love lives of his neighbors. He also marries a childlike woman named Dora, but she dies shortly after miscarrying their child. He goes to Europe for three years to recover from his grief and realizes he should have married his childhood friend Agnes, which he does after his return, and the two go on to have a happy life together. This novel explores some of the same themes as *Jane Eyre*, including poverty, abuse, schools, and marriage, but from a

British male perspective and with an unambiguously happy ending.

As for poets, Emily had wide-ranging taste. Keats was known for his reinvention of classic English poetic forms such as the sonnet. While not particularly prolific, he developed his style very quickly. He read countless ancient books and drew on many Greco-Roman traditions that went beyond his relatively limited literary education. Keats published several well-reviewed books of poetry in his lifetime.

Emerson is most often remembered for his speeches and lectures on world cultures, philosophy, and religion. He was famous across the country and frequently went on speaking tours to enthusiastic crowds. He was an outspoken champion of transcendentalism, which sees everything in nature as a tiny wonder, a version of the broader universe. Emerson was fascinated with India in particular, though he did not travel there and relied on reports from British colonists. As a poet, he was more melancholy and tried—and failed—to break from the conventions of meter and rhyme. However, his attempts helped later poets Walt Whitman and Emily Dickinson succeed in breaking the tight bonds of traditional poetic structure and introducing new kinds of poetry to America.

One of Emily's most cherished influences, Elizabeth Barrett Browning, was the more popular half of a poetry-writing couple. Her husband, Robert, also wrote poetry, but unusually for the period, she outshone him. Elizabeth was a social activist who used poetry to spread messages advocating against child labor, slavery, and oppression of minorities. She, like Keats and Dickinson, read widely in the Greco-Roman classics, and she became fluent in Greek and Latin to read famous texts in their original language. She published early and often and, after some missteps, was hailed as a great English poet in her own time. Browning experienced significant health issues and devastating family deaths, much like her younger poetic contemporary, but she continued writing. In contrast to Emily, she broke free from her domineering father to marry Robert Browning, and their marriage became a respectful and mutually beneficial partnership in writing and in life.

Emily had a curfew, and her father insisted that she maintain it. One night in 1851 after visiting with friends, Emily arrived home at nine o'clock to find her father furious with her. She considered leaving home, possibly to visit her brother, but she changed her mind. That evening, she wrote to Austin:

[I] found Father in great agitation at my protracted stay — and mother and Vinnie in tears, for fear that he would kill me. . . . I put on my bonnet tonight, opened the gate very desperately, and for a little while, the suspense was terrible — I think I was held in check by some invisible agent, for I returned to the house without having done any harm!

When Edward Dickinson was home, he demanded that the letters that Emily received be read aloud. This lack of privacy bothered Emily, who communicated frequently by letter. In October 1851, she wrote to Austin:

I received what you wrote, at about 2½ oclock yesterday. Father brought home the same, and waited himself in order to have me read it — I reviewed the contents hastily — striking out all suspicious places, and then very *artlessly* and unconsciously began. My heart went "pit a pat" till I got safely by a remark concerning Martha, and my stout heart was *not* till the manuscript was over. The allusion to Dick Cowles' grapes, followed by a sarcasm on Mr. Adams' tomatoes, amused father highly.

In 1850, the Amherst College newspaper, the *Indicator*, published a humorous valentine in the February issue. The valentine was playful, written in letter format, and unusually long for a valentine verse. Emily had written the work as a letter to her friend George Gould, who was an editor at the *Indicator*. It began with a nonsense verse that read:

Magnum bonum, "harum scarum," zounds et zounds, et war alarum, man reformam, life perfectum, mundum changum, all things flarum?

The letter continued by addressing the imaginary valentine directly. The speaker emphasizes that she does not care what her valentine wears, what weapons he carries, or how he travels. She cares only that they get to see each other. Emily uses the letter to poke fun at some of the conventions of valentines and courtship letters of the day.

> Sir, I desire an interview; meet me at sunrise, or sunset, or the new moon — the place is immaterial. In gold, or in purple, or sackcloth — I look not upon the *raiment*. With sword, or with pen, or with plough — the weapons are less than the *wielder*. In coach, or in wagon, or walking, the *equipage* far from the *man*. With soul, or spirit, or body, they are all alike to me. With host or alone, in sunshine or storm, in heaven or earth, *some* how or *no* how — I propose, sir, to see you.

The *Indicator* listed the author of the poem as "anonymous." But a comment accompanied the poem: "I wish I knew who the author is. I think she must have some spell, by which she quickens the imagination, and causes the high blood 'run frolic through the veins.'" It is unknown how the editor of that particular issue, Henry Shipley, got ahold of his friend George's letter and whether Emily was aware it would be published.

Emily loved to try her hand at writing valentines. It was common for young women of Amherst to use valentine writing as a way to show off their knowledge of literature and their creative wit. In 1852, one of Emily's whimsical valentine poems was published in the *Springfield Daily Republican*, a western Massachusetts newspaper read by people across the country.

This piece was to be the first "poem," in the traditional sense, of Emily's to be published, and one of only a handful published in her lifetime. Here, instead of nonsense verse, Emily used Latin phrases and poetic references to begin her work. The references scattered throughout the poem would have indicated to readers the poet's level of education and experience with history, science, and literature. Without background knowledge, it would have been difficult to appreciate or understand the work. However, the poem's humor and sarcasm actually end up mocking the very types of formal education it describes.

Sic transit gloria mundi
"How doth the busy bee"
Dum vivamus vivamus,
I stay mine enemy! —

Oh veni vidi vici!
Oh caput cap-a-pie!
And oh "memento mori"
When I am far from thee

Hurrah for Peter Parley
Hurrah for Daniel Boone
Three cheers sir, for the gentleman
Who first observed the moon —

Peter put up the sunshine!
Pattie arrange the stars
Tell Luna, tea is waiting
And call your brother Mars — . . .

Good bye Sir, I am going
My country calleth me
Allow me Sir, at parting
To wipe my weeping e'e

In token of our friendship
Accept this "Bonnie Doon"
And when the hand that pluck'd it
Hath passed beyond the moon

The memory of my ashes
Will consolation be
Then farewell Tuscarora,
And farewell Sir, to thee.

As talented as Emily was at writing light, sentimental, or silly valentine poems, she was also beginning to write more serious poetry. The next recorded poem of Emily's was written in 1853. It is a call to a godlike figure to "pilot" the speaker's soul over stormy seas to the "peaceful west" where they may rest for eternity—a far cry from the light, flirtatious words of a few years prior.

On this wondrous sea – sailing silently –
Ho! Pilot! Ho!
Knowest thou the shore
Where no breakers roar –
Where the storm is o'er?

In the silent West
Many – the sails at rest –
The anchors fast.
Thither I pilot thee –
Land! Ho! Eternity!
Ashore at last!

Emily often shared her poems with people whom she knew would support her, such as Benjamin Newton, a friend and an apprentice in her father's law office. Emily also exchanged poems with Henry Vaughan Emmons, a student at Amherst College, and Joseph Lyman, a friend of both Emily and Austin and a love interest of Emily's younger sister, Lavinia. Sue Gilbert was also a great support. Like Emily, Sue was well educated, intelligent, and interested in writing, and the two women were close friends. At Emily's request, Sue often critiqued Emily's poems. Sue even received a version of "On this wondrous sea" with an additional commanding opening line of "Write! Comrade, write!" In this way, poetry became a shared language between the two.

In September 1852, Sue accepted a teaching job in Baltimore, Maryland. Emily was devastated at losing the constant company of her friend. By the spring of 1853, Emily was experiencing pangs of loneliness. Sue was still in Baltimore, Austin was in Boston, and many of her childhood friends were no longer part of her life. Jane Humphrey had become a teacher and lived outside Amherst. Emily Fowler, Abiah Root, and Abby Wood had become engaged and married. Other friends, such as Jennie Grout and Martha Kingman, had fallen ill and died. Emily's social circle was becoming smaller and smaller with each passing year.

Emily's loss of close companions was not the only change happening in her life. Her mental state was in flux, and she felt a creeping sense of anxiety even in familiar settings. Still, Emily carried on with her day-to-day life as best she could. But one day in January 1854, Emily was on her way to church when suddenly and without warning a feeling of terror came over her. She couldn't find any reason for the fear, but it made her want to run for her life. In a letter to Sue, Emily described the event:

I'm just from meeting, Susie, and as I sorely feared, my "life" was made a "victim." I walked — I ran — I turned precarious corners — One moment I was not — then soared aloft like Phoenix, soon as the foe was by . . . I reached the steps, dear Susie. . . . How big and broad the aisle seemed, full huge enough before, as I quaked slowly up — and reached my usual seat!

In vain I sought to hide behind your feathers — Susie — feathers and *Bird* had flown, and there I sat, and sighed, and wondered I was scared so, for surely in the whole world was nothing I need to fear — Yet there the Phantom was, and though I kept resolving to be as brave as Turks, and bold as Polar Bears, it did'nt help me any.

Emily felt a sense of mortal danger. But she didn't know what the danger was from, since she realized that "in the whole world was nothing I need to fear." The "Phantom" was what caused her fear, but she could not identify what it was. Emily went on to tell Sue that she became calmer by the end of the church service, and she was content to walk home with her sister, Vinnie. Even then, she was a bit anxious.

> She [Vinnie] entertained me with much sprightly remark, until our gate was reached, and I need'nt tell you Susie, just how I clutched the latch, and whirled the merry key, and fairly danced for joy, to find myself *at home*!

Emily experienced a fear that was more terrifying than anything she had ever known. But she recognized that there was nothing around her that should cause her to experience this terror. She felt as though she had gone out of her body or ceased to exist—for "One moment I was not." Because of her fear, she felt as if she were totally alone in the world.

Emily almost certainly had an anxiety condition called panic disorder. Many people, then and now, have experienced this terrifying disorder. At the time, doctors had little understanding of mental illness or the brain. As it was more often diagnosed in women, the medical community simply termed it "female nerves."

A panic disorder is typically a lifelong condition that manifests in early adulthood—generally a person's early twenties. First, they will begin to experience more and more general anxiety without an identifiable cause. Eventually, they will experience their first panic attack. Symptoms of a panic attack can include trouble breathing, dizziness, sweating, nausea, feeling detached from one's body, or feeling under attack or on the brink of death. These attacks are, of course, frightening, but they are also completely unexpected. Some people with panic disorder have even experienced a panic attack when waking up from sleeping.

When someone has a panic attack in a certain place, they are

Emily greatly valued Sue Gilbert (*above*) for her literary and editorial opinions.

scared that if they return to that place, it will trigger another attack. This can lead to agoraphobia, or fear of areas one cannot easily escape. After her panic attack, Emily decided not to attend church anymore. She was afraid of reexperiencing the horror she faced on her way to church that day in January. Unfortunately, it would be the first of many places that would lose their sense of safety for her.

A few months later, Sue Gilbert returned to Amherst. Sue and Emily tried to renew the intimate friendship that they had before Sue had left. But something was different. Emily was hurt that her friend hadn't written as often or as passionately as Emily had. Sue, on the other hand, felt that Emily was too possessive with their friendship. Also, Sue was a devout churchgoer and proclaimed Christian, while Emily no longer went to church and had never been formally "saved." These differences led to a huge argument between the two. Finally, Emily wrote Sue a letter in which she expressed her feelings about the future of their relationship.

Sue — you can go or stay — There is but one alternative — We differ often lately, and this must be the last.

You need not fear to leave me lest I should be alone, for I often part with things I fancy I have loved, — sometimes to the grave, and sometimes to an oblivion rather bitterer than death — thus my heart bleeds so frequently that I shant mind the hemorrhage, and I only add an agony to several previous ones. . . .

SHE'S JUST HYSTERICAL: MISOGYNY IN WOMEN'S MENTAL HEALTH

The term *hysteria* has been used as a weapon against women for more than two thousand years. It comes from the Greek word *hysterikos*, meaning "a disturbance of the womb." The ancient Greeks believed certain psychological problems were unique to women and were caused by the womb shifting about in the body. This idea would carry through all the way to 1800s New England, where doctors still believed certain mental conditions were inherently female.

Treatments for these female conditions were experimental at best and cruel at worst. In the 1800s, upper-class women were often prescribed cold, fresh air and lots of bed rest. They might also take any number of untested concoctions with popular ingredients of the day like lead and mercury. Poorer women were often just committed to insane asylums by husbands, fathers, and sons who declared them unfit to live in society for all manner of reasons. Women could be committed for refusing their husbands, showing too much initiative, not adhering to social or societal standards of decency, or any other reason the men in their life could think up to get rid of them.

Given Emily's frequent writing of seeing specters and invisible forces around her, it is a wonder she was not committed herself. Some scholars argue this is part of why her father, Edward, refused to let the poet have more freedom and the Dickinson clan was so tight-knit. They might well have been trying to keep prying eyes from seeing signs other Amherst residents would deem as symptoms of hysteria.

But the problems in seriously considering women's health would long outlast the nineteenth century. The twentieth century gave rise to practices like lobotomy, electroshock therapy, isolation cells, and prescribed tranquilizers. All these practices were designed to make unhappy or uncooperative wives, daughters, and mothers calm and obedient, and all were capable of inflicting permanent brain damage on their victims. This legacy of pain is part of what makes Emily's poems on her own struggles with mental health just as poignant today as they were in the mid-nineteenth century.

Few have been given me, and if I love them so, that for *idolatry*, they are removed from me — I simply murmur *gone*, and the billow dies away into the boundless blue, and no one knows but me, that one went down today. We have walked very pleasantly — Perhaps this is the point at which our paths diverge — then pass on singing Sue, and up the distant hill I journey on.

The rift between the friends did not last long. In subsequent letters, Emily continued to express her longing to be with Sue. But Sue's affections were directed elsewhere. At the time, Sue was being courted by Austin. The pair were secretly engaged by 1853, and they planned to marry in the autumn of 1855. Although some of the intimacy was lost in Emily and Sue's relationship, Emily settled for having Sue as a future sister-in-law.

FIVE

I CAN LOVE YOU ANEW

BETWEEN THE LINES

One of the most enduring mysteries of Emily Dickinson's life is her perspective on romance. As a poet, Emily wrote a great deal about love, marriage, and sexual desire, but she remained unmarried and without children her entire life. Of course, this does not mean she did not experience love, requited or otherwise. Beyond her poetry, Emily's letters to a number of people in her life overflow with passion, declarations of love, and expressions of devotion. All these elements point to the famous "spinster recluse" having at least one, if not more than one, significant romantic relationship—but biographers have long wondered with whom.

Emily had crushes early in life on her teachers and fellow students, as many young people do, and was especially close to her early friend Abiah Root, often spending their free time together. Emily spoke in one of her letters to Abiah of being "always in love with [her] teachers" while at Amherst Academy. As she grew into her teens, the poet kept company with many of her brother's school friends and other local boys, although it's unclear if any of those attachments were romantic.

Two of Emily's close male friends in her teens and twenties have been suggested as potential love interests. The first is George Gould, a student at Amherst College who helped run the college's student newspaper the *Indicator*. He and Emily exchanged letters, but only her quirky valentine letter survived to see publication. However, there is evidence that he and Emily were very briefly engaged to be married. Whatever their relationship in the 1850s, by 1862 George was married and beginning a family of his own.

The other early male candidate for young Emily's

affections was her father's law clerk Benjamin Franklin Newton. Newton, as Emily referred to him in her letters, was definitely a mentor figure for the poet and provided her with new and challenging reading material. He also spent lots of time with the whole Dickinson family, often stopping by the Homestead to help Edward Dickinson with his work or just to spend time with Emily, Austin, and Lavinia. However, the evidence for Emily being in love with Newton is fairly scant. She did write a poem in his honor after his untimely death from tuberculosis, but she did the same for other friends she lost. Still, many scholars and adapters of Emily's continue to dwell on Newton as a potential love interest.

There are also two women suggested as romantic interests of Emily's during this same period. The lesser known of the two was Catherine "Kate" Turner. She came to Amherst in the mid-1800s with her new—but very ill—husband and became a widow just a few years later. Because she, Emily, and Susan Gilbert were all around the same age, they frequently socialized together. Kate shared Emily's passion for literature and a degree of mischief. However, we have no preserved correspondence between Kate and Emily. In fact, the only correspondence that survives is between Sue and Kate. This makes it difficult to determine the extent of their relationship.

Perhaps the most speculated and longest lasting of Emily's alleged romances was with her school friend and eventual sister-in-law, Susan Gilbert. Shortly after the two met in their last years at Amherst Academy, Emily was drawn to her witty, sharp-tongued classmate. Sue was popular in Amherst social circles and seemed to have a particularly strong hold over the Dickinson siblings. They were inexplicably fascinated by her, even when she showed no or little interest in return.

In her letters to Sue in the early 1850s, Emily expressed the intense depths of her feelings. She compared herself and Sue to famous lovers like Antony and Cleopatra. She drew on metaphors comparing Sue to God and to birds—a classic image male suitors used to describe the women they were interested in. She was also surprisingly direct and open with Sue in a way she was not with her other correspondents, even her beloved brother, Austin. In poems and letters sent to her absent Sue, Emily continually begs for her to come back.

Will you let me come dear Susie — looking just as I do, my dress soiled and worn, my grand old apron, and my hair — Oh Susie, time would fail me to enumerate my appearance, yet I love you just as dearly as if I was e'er so fine, so you wont care, will you? I am so glad dear Susie — that our hearts are always clean, and always neat and lovely, so not to be

Dickinson (*left*) with Kate Turner circa 1859

ashamed. I have been hard at work this morning, and I ought to be working now — but I cannot deny myself the luxury of a minute or two with you.

The dishes may wait dear Susie — and the uncleared table stand, *them* I have always with me, but you, I have "not always" — *why* Susie, Christ hath saints *manie* — and I have *few*, but thee — the angels shant have Susie — no — no no! . . . Oh my darling one, how long you wander from me, how weary I grow of waiting and looking, and calling for you; sometimes I shut my eyes, and shut my heart towards you, and try hard to forget you because you grieve me so, but you'll never go away, Oh you never will — say, Susie, promise me again, and I will smile faintly — and take up my little cross again of sad — *sad* separation. How vain it seems to *write*, when one knows how to feel — how much more near and dear to sit beside you, talk with you, hear the tones of your voice. . . . Only *want* to write me, only sometimes sigh that you are far from me, and that will do, Susie. . . . Love always, and ever, and true!

Emily —

IF YOU SAW A BULLET HIT A BIRD:
THE MASTER LETTERS

Before her death, Emily left certain letters on her desk with instructions to burn them. This was a common practice during the period, both to maintain the privacy of the deceased person's communications and to lessen the amount of letter sorting surviving loved ones had to complete. Vinnie respected her sister's wishes and immediately put this correspondence in the fire.

The younger sister found three letters that had not been marked for burning, however. Emily may have meant for these letters to be found or she may have forgotten about them. Those letters, the "Master" letters, were some of the longest letters that Emily had ever written. They are also clearly rough drafts, with insertions, crossed-out portions, and inkblots. Their existence is one of the mysteries of Emily Dickinson's life.

Scholars long assumed these were meant for a man that Emily was in love with, as the language has outpourings of love and desire. The question was, "Who is the person Emily addresses as 'Master'?" There were several men with whom Emily corresponded during her lifetime who were considered strong candidates. Among them were Samuel Bowles and Charles Wadsworth. The latter was suggested purely because Martha Dickinson Bianchi, Sue's daughter, suggested in an early memoir that her aunt was in love with the captivating minister and public speaker, despite the fact that Emily only saw him once while he was preaching and the few letters the two exchanged were clearly platonic.

The second part of the mystery concerns the dates that the letters were written. These dates may have given some clue as to the identity of the "Master," but Vinnie removed the dates from the remaining letters. Samuel Bowles was ruled out as "Master" after new scholarship on the potential dates of Emily's earliest drafts predated her meeting Samuel. They have been roughly dated to spring 1858, early 1861, and summer 1861.

The special quality of these letters is found in the intensity of feelings with which they were written. There is none of the light joking or happy affection of Emily's other poetry and letters. She is serious, melancholy, and sophisticated in her language.

Emily wrote with intense emotion:

This draft of one of the "Master" letters, written by Dickinson in about 1858, was left among her papers. It is unknown if a final copy was ever sent to the person addressed.

Master.

If you saw a bullet hit a Bird — and he told you he was'nt shot — you might weep at his courtesy, but you would certainly doubt his word.

One drop more from the gash that stains your Daisy's bosom — then would you *believe?* . . .

I am older — tonight, Master — but the love is the same — so are the moon and the crescent. If it had been God's will that I might breathe where you breathed — and find the place — myself — at night — if I (can) never forget that I am not with you — and that sorrow and frost are nearer than I. . . .

I want to see you more — Sir — than all I wish for in this world — and the wish — altered a little — will be my only one — for the skies.

Could you come to New England, [this summer — could] would you come to Amherst — Would you like to come — Master?

Sir — it were comfort forever — just to look in your face, while you looked in mine.

No one knows whether these letters were ever mailed. They may have been written by Emily for the purpose of writing down her pain and sorrow over a love that would never be returned, or they may have been a purely literary exercise to see what she was capable of. Whatever the reason, they are a striking example of her literary abilities and passionate voice in a pure, prose form.

In another letter to Sue Gilbert, Emily poured out more of her heart. In the first sentence of the letter, she quoted from Longfellow's poem "The Rainy Day."

It's a sorrowful morning Susie — the wind blows and it rains; "into each life some rain must fall," and I hardly know which falls fastest, the rain without, or within — Oh Susie, I would nestle close to your warm heart, and never hear the wind blow, or the storm beat, again. Is there any room there for me, or shall I wander away all homeless and alone? Thank you for loving me, darling, and *will* you "love me more if ever you come home"? — it is enough, dear Susie, I know I shall be satisfied. But what can I do towards you? — *dearer* you *cannot* be, for I love you so already, that it almost breaks my heart — perhaps I can love you *anew*, every day of my life, every morning and evening — Oh if you will let me, how happy I shall be!

The precious billet [letter], Susie, I am wearing the paper out, reading it over and o'er, but the dear *thoughts* cant wear out if they try, Thanks to Our Father, Susie! Vinnie and I talked of you all last evening long, and went to sleep mourning for you, and pretty soon I waked up saying "Precious treasure, thou art mine," and there you were all right, my Susie, and I hardly dared to sleep lest some one steal you away. Never mind the letter, Susie; you have so much to do; just write me every week *one line*, and let it be, "Emily, I love you," and I will be satisfied!

Your own Emily

Sue held a unique role as Emily's most frequent correspondent. Sue received far more letters and poems than anyone else in Emily's life throughout the more than three decades they knew each other. This is even more remarkable for the fact that Sue lived next door, making letters almost entirely unnecessary. Emily considered Sue her intellectual equal and respected Sue's opinion on her poetry. While Emily sent her work to several other people, she always finalized

JUST GALS BEING PALS: ROMANTIC FRIENDSHIP IN 1800S AMERICA

The idea of the romantic friendship was first popularized by Carroll Smith-Rosenberg in her article "The Female World of Love and Ritual: Relations between Women in Nineteenth-Century America." The piece, published in 1975, attempted to distinguish between close-knit, even physically affectionate ties between women that were accepted by society and the deviant sexual desires of actual lesbians.

The separation of men and women in fixed gender roles for everyday life was crucial. The homosocial environment such segregation created lent itself to consistent, deep, affectionate relationships between women. This was accepted in society and seen as normal expressions of love. They may have used language we now associate with romantic love, but to those women and their contemporaries, such expressions would have been normal and unproblematic to their roles as wives and mothers.

Much like romantic relationships between women today, women in romantic friendships wrote letters about how they missed holding, kissing, and talking to their friends. They might share beds, live together for extended periods, and play support roles for their friends' families. Women might also express fear or despair at the thought of marriage and separation from their friends. The relationships could span decades and marriages, births and deaths, as well as moves across the country. Romantic friendships could take place between relatives and could reflect either sisterly or mother-daughter bonds. These friendships not only helped young women practice the intimacy they would share with their future husbands but would provide mentorship and emotional connection in a world absent of men.

Although there were no doubt many intense, platonic friendships, it is misguided to assume all relationships of any period can be so easily categorized. It is just as likely that two women were in a romantic friendship in the 1800s as it was that they would use that societally acceptable notion to disguise a committed romantic, and perhaps sexual, relationship. While much has been made of reading too much into women's relationships in past time periods, there is just as much risk of erasing the people who were queer through the explanation, "They were just close friends."

her drafts before sending them. Sue was the only person who saw the poet's works in progress.

In one letter to Sue, Emily enclosed a poem that she addressed to her father but never gave to him. He often woke her early in the morning when she preferred to sleep in. Emily's willingness to share these tongue-in-cheek poems with Sue speaks to the familiarity of their relationship.

To my Father—
    to whose untiring efforts in my behalf, I am indebted for my *morning-hours*—viz—3. AM. to 12. PM. these grateful lines are inscribed by his aff
    Daughter.

> Sleep is supposed to be
> By the souls of sanity –
> The shutting of the eye.
>
> Sleep is the station grand
> Down wh' on either hand –
> The Hosts of Witness stand!
>
> Morning has not occurred!
>
> That shall Aurora be
> East of Eternity!
> One with the banner gay,
> One in the red array –
> *That* is the Break of Day!

We will never know who may have stolen Emily's heart during her young adulthood, but we do know that a variety of people influenced her during this critical time. Each one impacted her writing in the years following, and some became regular correspondents.

SUE, FOREVERMORE:
THE LIFE OF SUSAN HUNTINGTON
GILBERT DICKINSON

If someone in the twenty-first century has heard of Susan Dickinson, it is almost certainly because of her sister-in-law Emily. But despite the pair's closeness, Sue had a distinct life from the mysterious poet next door, both before and after Sue married Austin and officially joined the Dickinson family.

Susan Gilbert was born on December 19, 1830, just nine days after Emily. She; her parents, Harriet and Thomas; and her six older siblings lived about 20 miles (32 km) from Amherst, but Sue's childhood would be drastically different from those in the Dickinson family. When Sue was just seven years old, her mother died of tuberculosis. Sue's father, Thomas, an alcoholic tavern keeper with a debt problem, chose to send her and her sisters to live with their aunt in Geneva, New York, where Sue would return often throughout her life.

When Sue was eleven, her father died, leaving her and her siblings orphaned. She traveled back and forth between New York and Massachusetts growing up, visiting first her father and later her eldest sister, Harriet, in Amherst. When she finished schooling at Utica Academy in Utica, New York, Sue moved to live in Amherst full-time with Harriet and their other sister, Martha. Although Harriet and her store-owner husband were well off, he was not fond of his young sisters-in-law sharing their house, and Sue did not feel welcome there. That perhaps explains why she spent so much time at the Homestead and traveled to teach in her late teens and early twenties.

Not long after Sue finished her schooling, she became close friends with both Emily and Austin Dickinson. Despite both siblings vying for her attention, Austin eventually won out, and Sue agreed to Austin's marriage proposal in 1853. However, she would put off the actual wedding for three more years, safe in the knowledge that her brothers had provided several thousand dollars for her dowry from their remarkable financial success.

For the ceremony, she and Austin traveled back to Geneva, New York, to marry with her aunt and surviving siblings attending before they returned to Amherst once more. Then, married and moved into Austin's house next door to the Homestead—called the Evergreens—Sue began her role as wife and, eventually, mother.

One reason Sue was reluctant to marry was her fear of childbirth. Her sister Mary had died in childbirth just a year after her marriage. Some scholars and memoirs by Amherst residents suggest she performed several at-home abortions in a desperate attempt not to give birth, and she even held off on agreeing to marry Austin until he offered to not consummate their marriage right away. But pregnancy came anyway, and Sue had three children: Edward "Ned" Dickinson in 1861, Martha "Mattie" Dickinson in 1866, and Thomas Gilbert "Gib" Dickinson in 1875. She would cherish her children and mourn terribly when both her sons died—Gib in 1883 at just eight years old, and Ned in 1898 after struggling with ill health throughout his twenties and thirties.

Beyond her traditional roles as a wife and mother, Sue also took on the jobs of writer and town socialite. She was well connected to artists in New York, Massachusetts, and elsewhere, and she invited writers and public figures from all around to visit and speak at the Evergreens. Sue also had a few of her short stories and one poem, albeit more traditional than her sister-in-law's, published in newspapers. She was known for holding gorgeous, well-attended parties and seeing to all her guests with grace and elegance. In a very real sense, the Evergreens was the center of small-town Amherst's social life. However, the celebratory atmosphere would not last.

Although the relationships between Sue, her children, and her in-laws were strong and for the most part content, her marriage to Austin was fraying. Austin hired David Peck Todd as an astronomy professor at Amherst College in 1881. By the next year, Austin had begun a passionate thirteen-year affair with David's young wife, Mabel Loomis Todd, which would upend the lives and reputations of almost everyone in the Dickinson and Todd families. In 1883, when Sue's young son Gib died, her life was plunged into chaos. Austin's affair quickly became public knowledge, and Sue developed a new reputation as the grieving, angry, bitter wife of an unfaithful husband. However, she carried on trying to salvage her marriage and relationships with Lavinia and Emily and leaned on her surviving children, Ned and Mattie, for emotional support. Emily died in 1886, and Austin followed in 1895. Ned passed away three years later, and Lavinia died in 1900.

After the deaths of so many family members, Sue reinvented herself. She left Amherst, where she had been for so many years, and traveled. Before her death in 1913, Sue made numerous extended trips to Europe and spent much time with her daughter and only surviving child, Mattie, sharing stories of her time with the Dickinsons that Mattie would eventually publish in her memoir. As she differed from Emily in childhood, so did Sue differ in death, passing away at eighty-three years old as a well-traveled woman with a variety of life experiences.

SIX

I'LL TELL YOU WHAT I SEE TODAY

1855–1859

In early February 1855, Emily and Vinnie left on a trip to Washington, DC. This was the longest distance Emily had ever traveled from home, and initially she refused to go along. She and Vinnie were to spend three weeks in the nation's capital visiting their father. Since Edward Dickinson's election to Congress in 1852, he had spent a great deal of time traveling back and forth between Amherst and Washington.

Edward Dickinson was too busy with his congressional duties to show his daughters around the city, so Emily and Vinnie took themselves to see the sights. The two sisters also visited Philadelphia on their return trip home. Emily wrote to Elizabeth Holland, a woman she had met a few years earlier and with whom she had formed a close friendship, and told about her visit to the nation's capital:

> Philadelphia, 18 March 1855
> Dear Mrs. Holland and Minnie, and Dr. Holland too . . .
> I am not at home — I have been away just five weeks today, and shall not go quite yet back to Massachusetts. Vinnie is with me here, and we have wandered together into many new ways.
> We were three weeks in Washington, while father was there, and have been two in Philadelphia. We have had many pleasant times, and seen much that is fair, and heard much that is wonderful — many sweet ladies and noble gentlemen have taken us by the hand and smiled upon us pleasantly — and the sun shines brighter for our way thus far.

Vinnie Dickinson

I will not tell you what I saw — the elegance, the grandeur; you will not care to know the value of the diamonds my Lord and Lady wore, but if you haven't been to the sweet Mount Vernon, then I *will* tell you how on one soft spring day we glided down the Potomac in a painted boat, and jumped upon the shore — how hand in hand we stole along up a tangled pathway till we reached the tomb of General George Washington, how we paused beside it, and no one spoke a word, then hand in hand, walked on again, not less wise or sad for that marble story. . . .

Now, my precious friends, if you won't forget me until I get home, and become more sensible, I will write again, and more properly. Why didn't I ask before, if you were well and happy?

Forgetful
Emilie.

Emily and Vinnie enjoyed their trip despite the elder sister's anxiety about leaving home (and possibly having another panic attack). Emily's house on West Street was her sanctuary that she could always return to for safety. However, she would soon be forced to leave her safe place for another house, where she would remain for the rest of her life.

In April 1855, Edward Dickinson bought back the Dickinson Homestead, the house in which Emily had been born. For Edward, reclaiming the house his father had built was a way to reclaim the family's reputation. He also hoped the Homestead would become the permanent home for future generations of Dickinsons. He was therefore

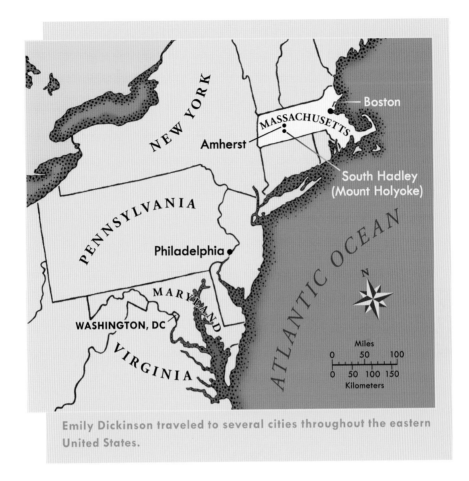

Emily Dickinson traveled to several cities throughout the eastern
United States.

not content to take the house as it was. He hired carpenters and painters
to expand and refurbish the buildings to a new level of grandeur. They
worked for several months readying the house for the Dickinson family,
and in November, the family moved in.

It was a difficult move, however, as Emily indicated in one of her
letters to Elizabeth Holland soon after the family was settled in their new
home. But Emily displayed humor in the face of a tough situation.

> Your voice is sweet, dear Mrs. Holland — I wish I heard it
> oftener. . . .
>
> I cannot tell you how we moved. I had rather not remember.
> I believe my "effects" were brought in a bandbox, and the

"deathless me," on foot, not many moments after. I took at the time a memorandum of my several senses, and also of my hat and coat, and my best shoes — but it was lost in the *mêlée*, and I am out with lanterns, looking for myself. . . .

From your mad
Emilie.

Emily's duties in her new home didn't change much from those in the old. Even though families as well off as the Dickinsons did not need the women of the house to do as much domestic labor as poorer families, there was still a good deal to be done. Emily, Vinnie, and their mother divided up the work, provided their mother was well. The family also had a hired servant, Irish immigrant Margaret O'Brien, who served the household from the mid-1850s to 1865, after which another Irish immigrant, Margaret Maher, took over and served until the 1890s. Maggie, as both women were referred to, substantially eased the workload of Vinnie and Emily, allowing Emily in particular more freedom and opportunity to write.

Emily's tasks included everything from baking bread daily to sweeping the kitchen, making the beds, and washing the floors on her hands and knees. However, she distinctly disliked cleaning chores and gravitated instead toward the kitchen. A cheerful place with pale green walls interrupted by yellow window casements, the kitchen was one of Emily's favorite rooms in the house. The many windows allowed the sunlight to shine into the room on bright, pleasant days. Compared to the cold, imposing brick of other areas of the house, the kitchen felt welcoming and warm.

Cooking and baking were some of Emily's favorite chores. A friend once commented that "she makes all the bread, for her father only likes hers." Emily's rye-and-Indian bread was so delicious that it took second prize at the 1856 Amherst Agricultural Fair. Emily's gingerbread was also a favorite in the Dickinson household.

Part of Emily's day was spent in the conservatory that lay next to the main house. There she nurtured herbs, wildflowers, and other plants. She also spent at least one hour each day of the summer tending the lush vegetable garden on the side of the house. Emily loved being outside and experiencing the richness of each season as it came and went. The open, inviting grounds may have helped Emily's anxiety and her difficulty settling back into a house she hadn't lived in for decades. In April 1856, Emily wrote about her delight

Edward Dickinson

in the outdoor world to her cousin John Graves.

It is Sunday — now — John — and all have gone to church — the wagons have done passing, and I have come out in the new grass to listen to the anthems.

Three or four Hens have followed me, and we sit side by side — and while they crow and whisper, I'll tell you what I see today, and what I would that you saw —

. . . the crumbling elms and evergreens — and *other* crumbling things — that spring, and fade, and cast their bloom within a simple twelvemonth — well — *they* are *here*, and skies on me fairer far than Italy. . . . And here are Robins — just got home — and giddy Crows — and Jays. . . . Here's a *bumblebee* — not such as *summer* brings — John — earnest, manly bees, but a kind of a Cockney, dressed in jaunty clothes. . . . Then there are *sadder* features — here and there, *wings* half gone to dust, that fluttered so, last year — a mouldering plume, an empty house, in which a bird resided. Where last year's flies, their errand ran, and last year's *crickets fell*!

DIGGING DEEPER:
EMILY DICKINSON'S GARDENS
AND CONSERVATORY

A quick glance through Emily's poetry catalog will reveal her love of nature and of flowers in particular. They take up a considerable amount of space in her writing, both as direct references and as metaphors and repeated symbols. She used flowers and plants to inform, inspire, and accompany her poetry.

When the Dickinson family moved back to the Homestead property in 1855, Edward built his nature-obsessed daughter her own narrow conservatory off a wing of the house. The small but bright, all-glass space would allow Emily to grow a variety of exotic and local plants year-round, as well as to have a place in the house all to herself. The Dickinson women also maintained an orchard, flower beds, and a small produce plot on the larger property. Emily Norcross Dickinson is credited with passing on her love and knowledge of plants to her daughters, even if they did not accept much else from her. Lavinia and Emily worked side by side in the dirt for decades, bringing gorgeous blooms and homegrown crops to life. Even after Emily's death, Vinnie tried to maintain the extensive gardens, even as they grew wilder and more tumultuous.

Emily was well known in Amherst as a gardener and amateur botanist in her time. Her love of nature and cultivation fit comfortably within the acceptable hobbies for upper-class, mid-nineteenth-century women, so Emily could openly revel in her gardening. In this way, her poetry and gardening served as complements to each other. One required isolation, concentration, and a wealth of imagery. The other was relaxing, bright, and inviting, drawing people in and pushing the poet outdoors. Emily would eventually combine these worlds, bringing some of her blooms up to her room and placing them on the sill there, kept warm by the small stove by her bed.

She was deeply inspired by her gardens and conservatory while writing. Emily used many specialized terms in her poetry that she learned from gardening manuals and her botany classes at Mount Holyoke and Amherst Academy. In some cases, her understandings were so specific that early scholars of her poetry misunderstood and misinterpreted her poems to mean something substantially different. Emily was likewise a master of the language of flowers. This code of different flowers holding different meanings would have been easily recognized by most of the people in Emily's life, particularly fellow women. Emily's surviving letters and poem scraps often had pinholes or other marks where she attached a flower from her conservatory, adding another dimension to the written text she supplied.

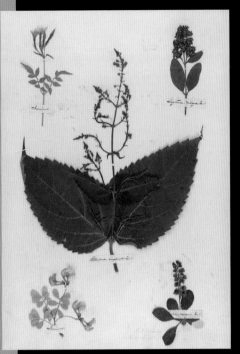

Many of the samples from Emily's herbarium came from the Homestead's gardens.

Sue was one of the most frequent flower recipients, likely partially because she lived next door and there was no fear the flower would be crushed on the journey, but also because Emily and Sue had a complex language of flowers all their own that Emily liked to reference in her accompanying poems to her sister-in-law. Emily also utilized the language of flowers with longtime correspondents Samuel Bowles, Judge Otis Lord, and Thomas Wentworth Higginson, as well as her cousins Loo and Fanny Norcross. Thomas, though, apparently did not always comprehend the poet's meaning. When she presented him with two daylilies on meeting him for the first time—meaning coquetry, or flirtatious behavior—he seemed confused. Writing to his wife later, he said her behavior was "like a child," which was pretty far from the cheeky introduction Emily likely hoped to convey.

By exploring Emily Dickinson's role as gardener as well as a poet, scholars and fans have found another way to connect and humanize her, as well as find avenues to explore her poetry anew.

In 1856 Austin married Sue Gilbert. Although Austin briefly considered moving with Sue to Chicago to start his own law firm, Edward Dickinson persuaded his son to stay in Amherst and work for him. In order to keep the family close by, he built a house next door to the Homestead. He called it the Evergreens because it was surrounded by immensely tall, ancient evergreen trees. The house was a grand-looking building designed in the style of an Italian villa. It stood in stark modern contrast to the solid, traditional brick of the Homestead next door. Austin and Sue moved in soon after their wedding.

It was wonderful for Emily to have both her brother and Sue living next door. The Evergreens became a social center where Austin and Sue hosted parties and literary events. Sue was a well-liked hostess with a reputation for throwing gatherings like a literary salon, an event where book lovers and authors came together to discuss the works of the day and share ideas.

At one such event, Emily met Ralph Waldo Emerson, an essayist and philosopher and the founder of the transcendentalist movement. Harriet Beecher Stowe, the author of *Uncle Tom's Cabin*, also visited the Evergreens from time to time. At her brother's house, Emily also met Samuel Bowles, the editor and sole writer of the *Springfield Daily Republican*. Samuel Bowles often visited not only Austin's home but Emily's as well.

Samuel was known for his appreciation of creative, intelligent women. He found both characteristics in Emily. He and Emily began

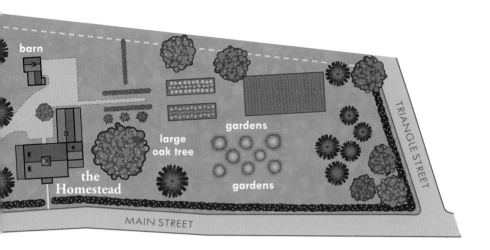

to write letters to each other. She also sent him many of her poems. Even though he had published one of her valentines several years earlier, Samuel did not really appreciate Emily's poetry. His taste in poetry ran to the conventional, and Emily's style was anything but conventional. Her poems did not adhere to rules of rhyme or verse, elements that were used to judge acceptable poems in the mid-1800s. Still, Emily persisted in sending letters and poetry anyway. Samuel became one of several people Emily would turn to for advice about her writing in the years to come.

Emily spent lots of time working on her poetry. She used any scrap of paper that was lying around, from recipe cards and envelopes to newspaper margins, to jot down the ideas that entered her head. Finally, Emily began to collect her poems into little notebooks, later termed fascicles. She painstakingly folded and sewed together pieces of paper to form a book. Then she would write one poem on each page.

As the year 1859 approached, Emily devoted more and more time to writing poetry. Sometimes she included one of her poems in a letter to a friend or to her sister-in-law, Sue. In December 1858, Emily wrote her sister-in-law a poem for her twenty-eighth birthday. In the piece, she emphasizes the similarities and differences between the Dickinsons by blood and Sue, a Dickinson by marriage. The poem exudes affection and love toward one of the most cherished people in Emily's life. In the final lines, the poet claims her sister-in-law as her own, acknowledging that whether by friendship, marriage, or love, the two will always be bound together.

> One Sister have I in the house -
> And one a hedge away.
> There's only one recorded -
> But both belong to me.
>
> One came the road that I came -
> And wore my last year's gown -
> The other, as a bird her nest
> Builded our hearts among.
>
> She did not sing as we did -
> It was a different tune -
> Herself to her a music
> As Bumble bee of June.

Emily often repurposed paper scraps for her manuscripts, such as this used envelope.

> Today is far from childhood,
> But up and down the hills,
> I held her hand the tighter -
> Which shortened all the miles -
>
> And still her hum
> The years among,
> Deceives the Butterfly;
> And in her Eye
> The Violets lie,
> Mouldered this many May -
>
> I split the dew,
> But took the morn -
> I chose this single star
> From out the wide night's numbers -
> Sue - forevermore!

ORDER FROM CHAOS: RECONSTRUCTING EMILY DICKINSON'S POETRY FASCICLES

When Lavinia Dickinson discovered her sister's trunk of poetry, she found more than just scraps of paper. In the chest were some forty small, handmade notebooks bound with thread. These notebooks were dubbed "fascicles," from the word for a section of a book published in parts. Dickinson did not intend to turn her notebooks into a published book, but the name stuck.

Why do readers not find Dickinson's work organized by fascicle? Because of her early editors, particularly Mabel Loomis Todd. Although Todd kept Dickinson's poems in their fascicles at first, she later unbound the notebooks to sort and rearrange them by theme. In the 1890s, when the first collection of Dickinson's poetry was published, readers expected poems to be organized into thematic categories. Accordingly, Todd did what she deemed necessary to get Dickinson's work published.

Decades later, an attempt was made to reconstruct the original fascicles. Scholars studied handwriting, paper and ink stains, the angle and size of holes punched for binding, and other physical clues. They also used some of Todd's early transcripts of parts of the fascicles. In 1981 R. W. Franklin released the first full attempt at reproducing Dickinson's original order, complete with facsimiles of the original notebooks.

Even after decades of research, there were questions about the fascicles' purpose. Were they for Dickinson's private use? Do they follow themes or an artistic layout, or is the order at random? Can they provide clues to the meaning behind some of Dickinson's more obscure poems?

According to Franklin, there does not appear to be a thought-out plan behind the fascicles. The earliest fascicles were the neatest with final copies of every poem on embossed paper. As the years went by and Dickinson started writing more and more poems, the fascicles became sloppier. These notebooks included many revisions and alternate word choices for poems, as well as extra poems tacked onto a partially finished notebook and rebound. The last fascicle is from 1864. Dickinson continued copying her poetry onto clean paper but never bound them.

SEVEN

THE MIND IS SO NEAR ITSELF

1860–1863

Emily continued to spend much of her time reading. She read some books over and over, quoting them in her letters to friends and family. Several poets, novelists, and essayists captured Emily's fancy. When Elizabeth Barrett Browning died in 1861, Emily felt as though she had lost a friend. As with Charlotte Brontë's heroine, Jane Eyre, Emily felt a kinship with Aurora Leigh, the heroine of Browning's verse novel. Published in 1856, *Aurora Leigh* is the story of a young woman who decides to become a poet instead of fulfilling the conventional role of wife. Aurora rejected a marriage proposal, knowing her suitor wanted to tie her down to house and family.

Emily certainly related to Aurora's desire to be seen as a poet. Her father and many others in Amherst did not see the value in women writing anything other than social letters. It's unclear whether Emily wanted her poems published, but she was definitely eager to share them. She sent hundreds of poems to close friends, casual acquaintances, and relatives. Emily often jumped straight from the prose of an ordinary letter into a work of poetry and then back to prose. These letter-poems, as they came to be known, reveal Emily's irresistible pull toward poetry.

Emily' read the *Springfield Daily Republican* every day. She was close with the editor, Samuel Bowles, and used his newspaper to stay informed about the politics and events of the time. Emily had mailed many poems to Mr. Bowles, either as parts of letters or for feedback, but aside from her valentine verses she had not seen one in print. Then, in May 1861, as Emily turned the pages of the *Republican*, she saw one of her poems. Everyone in her New England community would soon be reading her words.

I taste a liquor never
 brewed -
From Tankards scooped
 in Pearl -
Not all the Frankfort
 Berries
Yield such an Alcohol!

Inebriate of air - am I -
And Debauchee of Dew -
Reeling - thro' endless
summer days -
From inns of molten Blue - . . .

Between caring for her
mother, struggling with her
mental health, and dedicating
significant time to writing,
Emily began to spend
more and more time at the
Homestead.

Emily was working hard at her poetry despite trying circumstances. The Dickinson home was under a cloud of concern since Emily Norcross Dickinson had taken to her bed again, likely with a case of depression. Emily and Vinnie worried about their mother's health, and the household work fell on their servant Maggie's and their shoulders. Vinnie often took over Emily's tasks so her sister could draft poems and letters. Throughout their teens and adulthood, Vinnie gradually became more of a parent to Emily than their mother and father ever had been. Emily looked to Vinnie as her protector, confidant, and adviser. Vinnie fully accepted the role and guarded her sister against the outside world.

In the summer of 1861, Emily sent Sue a poem and asked for her opinion. This is the only direct surviving example of Sue serving as Emily's critic.

Safe in their Alabaster Chambers.
Untouched by morning
And untouched by noon,
Sleep the meek members of the Resurrection,
Rafter of satin
And Roof of stone.

Light laughs the breeze
In her Castle above them,
Babbles the Bee in a stolid Ear,
Pipe the Sweet Birds in ignorant cadence, –
Ah, what sagacity perished here!

While there is no record of Sue's reply, she must have been dissatisfied with the second verse, as Emily then sent her a revision of the poem:

Safe in their Alabaster Chambers,
Untouched by Morning—
And untouched by Noon—
Lie the meek members of the Resurrection –
Rafter of Satin – and Roof of Stone –

Grand go the Years – in the Crescent – about them –
Worlds scoop their Arcs –
And Firmaments – row –
Diadems – drop – and Doges– surrender –
Soundless as dots – on a Disc of Snow –

Sue responded quickly:

I am not suited dear Emily with the second verse – It is remarkable as the chain lightening that blinds us hot nights in the Southern sky but it does not go with the ghostly shimmer of the first verse as well as the other one – It just occurs to me that the first verse is complete in itself it needs no other, and can't be coupled – Strange things always go alone – as there is only one Gabriel and one Sun – You never made a peer for that verse, and I *guess* you[r] kingdom does'nt hold one – I always go to the fire and get warm after thinking of it, but I never *can* again . . .
 Sue –
Pony Express

A HARD ACT TO FOLLOW: LAVINIA DICKINSON'S LIFE AND LEGACY

It's hard coming last. And when you are the last sibling in a famous family, it is almost impossible not to be permanently defined by your better-known brother and sister. Lavinia "Vinnie" Dickinson ended up serving as her older sister Emily's support system, as well as her biggest champion after Emily's death. Though the two sisters were radically different from each other and further apart in age than Emily and Austin, Vinnie made crucial contributions to the poet's life.

Lavinia Norcross Dickinson was born February 28, 1833. It was a difficult birth, and Emily's mother spent some time in recovery and possible postpartum depression. The family was also in tough financial straits while Vinnie was a baby. Lavinia, like Emily, attended Amherst Academy, although she cared much less for formal education than her sister did. She attended Ipswich Academy only briefly after her regular schooling.

The youngest Dickinson was by far the liveliest, taking part in a wide variety of social events across Amherst and eventually entertaining many different suitors that came to call. One of these men, her brother Austin's friend Joseph Lyman, was the closest Lavinia ever got to marriage. The two were often seen together, and Vinnie was not shy about her love for Joseph. Years later in a letter to his wife, Joseph would look back fondly on the many sweet kisses and rendezvous that he and Lavinia had shared. He did propose to Vinnie, but for reasons that are not entirely clear, the two never married. Emily's little sister would also remain unmarried and childless her whole life and would dote heavily on her niece and nephews.

Martha Dickinson Bianchi, Sue and Austin's only daughter and Vinnie's only niece, would describe her younger aunt's unwavering devotion to caring for her big sister. Lavinia took on many of the boring, practical tasks of managing the Dickinson household and lived with her sister in the Homestead until the latter's death. Although Martha was quick to point

Vinnie Dickinson was instrumental in achieving the posthumous publication of her sister's poems.

out that Lavinia never expressed disappointment or anger toward Emily at essentially having to put her own life on pause, she wrote in her 1924 memoir: "If Emily had been less Emily, Lavinia might have been more Lavinia. As it was, Lavinia carried the family honor to her grave as a sacred but rather acrid burden."

After Emily died and Vinnie discovered the poetry her sister had left behind, she became determined to publish it. She aggressively worked to convince family friends and publishers that Emily's poetry needed to be heard by the world, and she financed the first printing of Emily's posthumous *Poems* herself. Finally, in 1899, Lavinia died, having outlived her parents, older siblings, close cousins, and both nephews. She was remembered fondly in the Amherst community and by her niece for her funny, charming personality; loyalty; and social graces.

A year later, the first version of this poem would be published in the *Springfield Daily Republican* with an added title. Sue, who had a poem published on the same page, wrote to Emily asking if she had seen the paper. Both poems were published anonymously.

In September 1861, Emily experienced another panic attack. A year later, she told her new correspondent and mentor Thomas Higginson: "I had a terror – since September – I could tell to none – and so I sing, as the Boy does by the Burying Ground – because I am afraid –"

Emily was slowly retreating from Amherst society. Some scholars consider this Emily's decision to focus on her poetry—the year 1862 being the most prolific of her lifetime and resulting in hundreds of poems. But it is likely her mental health was also a barrier. There were no treatments for panic disorders in mid-1800s Massachusetts. Further, upper-class people were not supposed to talk about terrors and visions of death. For this reason, Emily may have felt isolated, and she began to rely more heavily on written communication and her loved ones at home for support.

During this difficult time Emily began to write poetry about the joy and pain of being in love. In a poem written in 1861, Emily expressed her willingness to give up everything for the sight of her beloved's face.

> What would I give to see his face?
> I'd give - I'd give my life - of course -
> But *that* is not enough!
> Stop just a minute - let me think!
> I'd give my biggest Bobolink!
> That makes *two - Him -* and *Life*!
> You know who "*June*" is -
> I'd give *her* -
> Roses a day from Zinzebar -
> And Lily tubes - like wells -
> Bees - by the furlong -
> Straits of Blue -
> Navies of Butterflies - sailed thro' -
> And dappled Cowslip Dells - . . .

Love would come to be one of the poet's most frequently chosen subjects, alongside death, nature, and the workings of the mind.

In April 1862, thirty-one-year-old Emily was reading the *Atlantic Monthly*, one of the magazines delivered to the Dickinson home. An essay by Thomas Wentworth Higginson titled "Letter to a Young Contributor" expressed the sadness of a young editor who had to reject so many works submitted by both male and female poets.

"Letter to a Young Contributor" caught Emily's attention. The author knew that women could be fine poets and explained that editors are always hungering for new poems to publish. Emily decided that perhaps her poetry was just what the editor was looking for.

Emily wrote Mr. Higginson a letter of introduction in which she asked him to review her poetry, if he had the time. She enclosed four of her poems with the letter—"Safe in their Alabaster Chambers," "The nearest Dream recedes unrealized," "We play at Paste," and "I'll tell you how the Sun rose." She was so close to her poems that it was difficult for her to know whether they were good or not. She asked Thomas to let her know what he thought.

Mr Higginson,

Are you too deeply occupied to say if my Verse is alive?

The Mind is so near itself — it cannot see, distinctly — and I have none to ask —

Should you think it breathed — and had you the leisure to tell me, I should feel quick gratitude —

If I make a mistake — that you dared to tell me — would give me sincerer honor — toward you —

I enclose my name — asking you, if you please — Sir — to tell me what is true?

That you will not betray me — it is needless to ask — since Honor is it's own pawn —

Emily did not sign this letter. Instead, she included a card in its own envelope on which she wrote her name.

POOR LITTLE HEART!:
EMILY DICKINSON'S LOVE POETRY

For a woman with no official romantic attachments, Emily Dickinson wrote a lot about love. In fact, besides nature and death, it is one of her most frequent subjects. Her love poems are often short and cover a wide range of approaches, from childhood love lost and remembered to anguish of unrequited love to passionate, sensual expressions of desire. She offers many different ways to look at love, which partially explains their continued popularity for a wide variety of audiences.

In poems such as "The Moon is distant from the Sea," Dickinson utilizes her wealth of knowledge on the natural world to relate love to natural phenomena. That particular poem envisions the speaker as the sea, constantly and gently tugged on by the moon to create the tides. The "Signore" of the poem has full control of the speaker, who is "Obedient to the least command / Thine eye impose on me -" In three short stanzas, the tide has been transformed into communication and obedience between lovers.

Mr. Higginson was fascinated by Emily's unusual letter and her poetry. He had to know the person who could write like this. He hurriedly wrote a letter to Emily, asking all sorts of personal questions about her and her family life. He also gave some rather pointed criticism about the poems she had sent him, particularly about how they deviated from the conventional poetry formats of the time.

In her second letter to Thomas, on April 25, Emily enclosed a short poem in which she described her poems as flowers that she was presenting to him.

> South winds jostle them -
> Bumblebees come -
> Hover - hesitate -
> Drunk, and are gone -

Dickinson also liked to use and reuse specific images and analogies in her love poems. In several pieces, she creates a first-person perspective of an earl or duke. These viewpoints allow the poet to address a female subject with open love and desire, as in "The Malay - took the Pearl." The poem only just barely conceals the erotic nature by calling a woman a "pearl" that another man (Black, in a rather racist depiction) who is braver than the earl carries home and thoroughly enjoys. The earl is left behind, heartbroken, cursing himself for not acting on his love. A similar poem, "No matter – now – Sweet," has the speaker scolding their love interest for not sparing a smile or kind word of love for "that dull Girl," following with "But wont you wish you'd spared one / When I'm Earl?" Here, gender is twisted between the speaker's childhood (when she was a "dull Girl") and adulthood (as the masculine "Earl").

Finally, some poems have an eroticism that cannot be contained, despite the protests and excuses of Dickinson's early editors. One of the most famous is "Wild nights – Wild nights!" in which Dickinson uses a sailing metaphor to speak of love and passion, "Might I but moor – tonight – / In thee!"

Butterflies pause
On their passage Cashmere -
I - softly plucking,
Present them here!

In the letter, Emily thanked him for "the surgery—it was not so painful as I supposed." She agreed to send him more poems. Emily avoided sharing her age, although he had asked it. At thirty-one, Emily was past the age when most women in Amherst married and had children. She may have feared that Thomas would judge her for focusing on poetry instead of the standard roles for women of the period. Emily implied she was new to writing poetry, though by this point she had written nearly one thousand poems. This may have been to avoid criticism based on her gender. She also told him about her family and the books she enjoyed.

WILL YOU BE MY PRECEPTOR?: THOMAS WENTWORTH HIGGINSON AND THE CIVIL WAR

Although he did not enter Emily Dickinson's life until both were in their thirties, Thomas Higginson's upbringing shaped the man he became and the decades-long mentor Emily respected and admired. He was born in 1823 to his fiscally irresponsible father, Stephen, and Stephen's second wife, Louisa Storrow. Thomas's father helped create the Harvard Divinity School, the religious opposite of Calvinist Amherst College, and his poor management of the school's money would lead to financial problems for the Higginsons for the next decade.

However, being in the college town of Cambridge, Massachusetts, also gave young Thomas great access to knowledge, notable contemporary figures, and a wide variety of classes and books. By the time he was thirteen, Thomas was enrolled at Harvard College as an awkward 6-foot-tall (1.8 m) boy with little experience socializing with men much older than him. Eventually he made a few friends who introduced him to several prominent writers of the day, such as Ralph Waldo Emerson and the Brownings.

Unsure what to do after graduation, Thomas took a short-lived teaching post, then a job as a private tutor for three of his rich cousin's sons. He also toyed with the idea of being a writer—until Emerson himself reviewed his poems and told him they were not up to snuff. Thomas tried opium, just in case it unlocked some great writer within, and then gave up and went back to just reading other people's work. Soon after, he became engaged to his second cousin Mary Channing, and they were married in 1847.

During this time, Thomas was also developing his support for abolitionism and his outrage at the institution of slavery. After passing his classes at the Harvard Divinity School on his second try, Thomas and his new wife Mary set out to various New England towns where he would preach. He often included messages about the evils of slavery, and even tried to run for Congress to address the issue there. He also became involved in the early women's rights movement and women's suffrage. Thomas was lofty in his ideals and almost never practical, but he was working for change in a time when it was dangerous to speak up. He even took on daring—if ill-advised—plans to free imprisoned runaway enslaved people that in some cases involved little more than a battering ram and a few hand axes to take down the courthouse doors.

In 1858, after more failed attempts to free prisoners of various movements and to help Kansas homesteaders, Thomas left the church and began writing essays for the *Atlantic Monthly*. He worked as a writer there until the beginning of the Civil War, in which he quickly

Thomas Wentworth Higginson

enlisted. Thomas was quickly becoming noticed in New England for his writing and efforts in the Union army. He rose through the ranks and was appointed colonel of the first officially authorized regiment of freed slaves, named the First South Carolina Volunteers.

Thomas took to the role with enthusiasm, making sure his men were trained, well fed, and respected as much as possible by their fellow, white soldiers. However, he and his soldiers faced incredible racism within the Union army. Black soldiers had their pay cut, then had it withheld, were refused adequate medical treatment, and were put in some of the most dangerous positions in battle. Higginson, ever the activist, publicly berated the army in letters to both government offices and newspapers like the *New York Times*, decrying the practices. He grew disillusioned and eventually sick, taking a furlough and being diagnosed with malaria. In 1863 he resigned from the army and his post as colonel of the First Volunteers.

As Emily's life was largely untouched by the day-to-day realities of the Civil War—her brother having paid for a draft replacement and the biggest battles taking place far from Amherst—her new friend Thomas Higginson provided a valuable window into the extraordinary suffering the war produced. Emily wrote several poems on soldiers and the military during the years of the Civil War, and a few were published in local papers. Thomas had firsthand insight into a world Emily could not have ever participated in, sparking her imagination and her compassion for the cause.

Mr. Higginson,

. . . You inquire my Books – For Poets – I have Keats – and Mr and Mrs Browning. For Prose – Mr Ruskin – Sir Thomas Browne – and the Revelations.

. . . I have a Brother and Sister – My Mother does not care for thought – and Father, too busy with his Briefs – to notice what we do – He buys me many Books – but begs me not to read them – because he fears they joggle the Mind. They are religious – except me. . . .

You speak of Mr Whitman – I never read his Book – but was told that he was disgraceful –

I read Miss Prescott's "Circumstance," but it followed me, in the Dark – so I avoided her. . . .

Is this – Sir – what you asked me to tell you?

Your friend,

E – Dickinson.

Here, Emily refers to Walt Whitman's reputation as "disgraceful," as his prose poetry book *Leaves of Grass* was considered scandalous for his day and rumors circulated about him having sexual relationships with men. Ironically, Whitman and Dickinson would later be grouped together as two of the most influential poets of the nineteenth century for their groundbreaking poetic styles, and both would have their legacies as queer icons celebrated.

Emily told Higginson she had come across his essay in the *Atlantic Monthly*. She asked him to be her writing teacher. "I would like to learn – Could you tell me how to grow – or is it unconveyed – like Melody – or Witchcraft?"

Higginson, like Emily, delighted in the beauties of nature. Emily had read his four nature essays in the *Atlantic Monthly*. He had spent time with Henry David Thoreau, who had written *Walden*, a book about living a simple life in harmony with nature. Their shared love for nature may have been what bonded Emily and Higginson's friendship.

One of Emily's poems that Higginson enjoyed was dedicated to the months of March and April. Emily had written poems for all the months of the year, but she told Higginson this was her favorite:

Dear March - Come in -
How glad I am -
I hoped for you before -
Put down your Hat -
You must have walked -
How out of Breath you are -
Dear March, how are you, and the Rest -
Did you leave Nature well -
Oh March, Come right up stairs with me -
I have so much to tell -

I got your Letter, and the Birds -
The Maples never knew that you were coming -
I declare - how Red their Faces grew -
But March, forgive me -
All those Hills you left for me to Hue -
There was no Purple suitable -
You took it all with you -

Who knocks? That April -
Lock the Door -
I will not be pursued -
He stayed away a Year to call
When I am occupied -
But trifles look so trivial
As soon as you have come

That Blame is just as dear as Praise
And Praise as mere as Blame -

EIGHT

I FIND ECSTASY IN LIVING

1864–1870

One day when Emily was working on a poem, the page she was writing on began to blur. Emily panicked. Unlike the unexplainable fear of her panic attacks, the basis for this fear was tangible. Emily's sight was fading.

There was a history of poor eyesight in the Dickinson family. Both Vinnie and Emily Norcross Dickinson suffered from eye problems. At various times in their lives, their eyes became extremely sensitive to light and they had periods of blurred vision.

In February 1864, when Emily was thirty-three years old, she went with Vinnie to Boston to consult with an ophthalmologist. After a lengthy and careful examination, eye specialist Dr. Henry Willard Williams told Emily that he could probably treat her condition. She would have to return to Boston in April and remain there for seven months for treatments. While medical knowledge of the time was still a bit shaky and it is difficult to diagnose conditions from letters alone, Dickinson scholars think Emily likely had a type of eye inflammation that made her eyes sensitive to light, irritated, and difficult to focus.

After Emily returned to Amherst, she worried she might be losing her sight permanently. Although Dr. Williams recommended that she rest her eyes frequently and avoid reading and writing, Emily did none of these things. She began to write feverishly. She worked late at night and early in the morning, when the rest of the house was asleep and she was free from her household work. Emily had written hundreds of poems, but she wanted to revise many of them. With a feverish energy and the sense that time was running out on her, Emily continued to rewrite old poems and create new ones.

Then, on March 12, Emily discovered that the *New York Round Table* had printed one of her poems. This particular work reflected Emily's attitude toward her faith and organized religion. Instead of going to Sunday services, the poem's speaker finds God in nature, recognizing the holy elements of the everyday world.

Some keep the Sabbath going to Church -
I keep it, staying at Home -
With a Bobolink for a Chorister -
And an Orchard, for a Dome -

Some keep the Sabbath in Surplice -
I, just wear my Wings -
And instead of tolling the Bell, for Church,
Our little Sexton - sings.

God preaches, a noted Clergyman -
And the sermon is never long,
So instead of getting to Heaven, at last -
I'm going, all along.

On March 30 Emily saw another one of her poems in the *Springfield Daily Republican*. Again, the poem celebrated the beauty of nature's phenomena that others may take for granted.

Blazing in Gold and quenching in Purple
Leaping like Leopards to the Sky
Then at the feet of the old Horizon
Laying her Spotted Face to die
Stooping as low as the Otter's Window
Touching the Roof and tinting the Barn
Kissing her Bonnet to the Meadow
And the Juggler of Day is gone

The publication of these two poems was a bright spot in the midst of her troubles.

In April, Vinnie accompanied her sister back to Boston and settled her in with their cousins, Frances "Fanny" Norcross and Louise "Loo" Norcross, in nearby Cambridge. Their mother was the aunt whom Emily had stayed with as a toddler and remained close to throughout her childhood. Aunt Lavinia had died the year before, and her daughters lived in a boardinghouse. Emily was close to her cousins and was deeply affected by the loss of her aunt. The pair had visited Emily in Amherst after their mother had died, and Emily remained close with them.

Emily wrote to Vinnie from Cambridge about the treatment for her eyes.

Dear Vinnie,

I miss you most, and I want to go Home and take good care of you and make you happy every day.

The Doctor is not willing yet, and He is not willing I should write. He wrote to Father, himself, because He thought it not best for me.

You wont think it strange any more, will you?

Loo and Fanny take sweet care of me, and let me want for nothing, but I am not at Home, and the calls at the Doctor's are painful, and dear Vinnie, I have not looked at the Spring.

Wont you help me be patient?

I cannot write but this, and send a little flower, and hope you wont forget me, because I want to come so much I cannot make it show.

Emily.

In a letter to Higginson in early June, Emily hinted that she was told not to write for a while, but that she had defied the doctor's orders. "Can you render my Pencil? The Physician has taken away my Pen." The remark is literal as well as figurative—Emily switched from using ink pens to using pencil for both her letter writing and poetry from 1863 to 1865.

Emily did not return home again until just before Thanksgiving. Her eyes were sensitive to light, but she was trying to live her normal life. Still, Vinnie did try to prevent Emily from taking on too much eyestrain by insisting she do fewer detail-oriented tasks like sewing.

Emily stayed with her Norcross cousins near Boston to attend her eye treatments with Dr. Williams.

In a letter to her cousin Loo a few weeks after she returned home, Emily wrote about her activities:

> All that my eyes will let me shall be said for Loo, dear little solid gold girl. . . .
>
> You persuade me to speak of my eyes, which I shunned doing, because I wanted you to rest. I could not bear a single sigh should tarnish your vacation, but, lest through me one bird delay a change of latitude, I will tell you, dear.
>
> The eyes are as with you, sometimes easy, sometimes sad. I think they are not worse, nor do I think them better than when I came home.
>
> The snow-light offends them, and the house is bright; notwithstanding, they hope some. For the first few weeks I did nothing but comfort my plants, till now their small green cheeks are covered with smiles.

Emily returned to Boston in April 1865 for another eye examination. Her eyes were still sensitive to sunlight, but she decided not to consult any more doctors. She stayed in Cambridge for treatment for another few months before returning to Amherst in October. Her doctor suggested a third visit, but Emily hoped that the condition would clear up on its own. Her father, Edward, was also skeptical of letting his daughter leave home for yet another trip. Fortunately, her condition eased, and within the span of a year, Emily regained full use of her eyes.

The list of authors whose books Emily considered worthwhile reading grew shorter as the years went by. But one author stood out over all the rest in Emily's opinion: William Shakespeare. After she had returned from Boston, her eyes had improved enough that she could read again. Emily rejoiced. She decided to read a collection of Shakespeare's plays. Although Emily had studied Shakespeare while a student at Amherst Academy and as part of the informal Shakespeare Club, it had been years since she had focused intently on the bard's plays and poetry. She was filled with a new appreciation for his writing and felt that a person needn't read anyone else but Shakespeare to fulfill their literary needs.

> How my blood bounded! Shakespeare was the first . . . I thought why clasp any hand but this? Give me ever to drink of this wine. Going home I flew to the shelves and devoured the luscious passages. I thought I should tear the leaves out as I turned them, Then I settled down to a willingness for all the rest to go but William Shakespeare.

Emily's newfound love of Shakespeare's work was soon reflected in her poems and letters. She was quite fond of referencing the work of other writers in her own writing, and the references to Shakespeare grew considerably after 1865. Although Emily wrote fewer letters during the next four years, she maintained contact with Thomas Wentworth Higginson, her mentor. She continued to send him two or three of her poems with each letter.

In February 1866, Emily noticed one of her poems on the front page of the *Republican*. Free of the intense emotion often seen in Emily's poems, it read:

IMPERFECT HINDSIGHT: EXPLANATIONS OF EMILY DICKINSON'S HEALTH PROBLEMS

Emily Dickinson was ill for one reason or another for large stretches of her adult life. However, due to the constraints of medical knowledge of the day and a lack of her formal medical records, historians have to guess at what many of those ailments may have been. Emily's eye problems in her thirties, however, have been fairly consistently diagnosed as iritis. The condition is an inflammation around the iris, which causes considerable pain, temporary vision loss, and sensitivity to light. If not treated properly, iritis can cause permanent blindness.

When treated, iritis typically appears for a few months and then fades away. But the eye or eyes can get reinflamed, restarting the cycle. There are several ways that someone can contract iritis, although doctors are still uncertain on some details of this rare condition. One way to contract it is through infections like tuberculosis, syphilis, or toxoplasmosis. Tuberculosis was quite common in Amherst around the time when Emily experienced her eye problems, and some scholars have diagnosed an earlier period of sickness in Emily's twenties as tuberculosis. Iritis can also be caused by a genetic predisposition that runs in the family. Lavinia and Emily Norcross Dickinson also experienced some eye troubles in their lifetimes, though we have fewer details of their conditions.

Thankfully for her and for the poetry world, Emily recovered her sight. This was due in large part to her doctor, Dr. Henry Willard Williams, who actually wrote a paper in 1856 on his new methods of treating iritis without mercury. As we now know, mercury is a neurotoxin that damages human nervous systems and can lead to death. Emily was fortunate to be placed in the care of a doctor innovating in the condition with which she would come to him for help. Some have suggested that Emily's eye problems were part of her mental health struggles and were all in her head. We do not have concrete proof of this theory, but in any case, Dr. Williams had also treated patients with mental health problems that caused them to believe they were sick without any physical symptoms. Whatever the exact cause, by 1866 Emily had recovered and stayed in Amherst, taking in the visual beauty of her surroundings once again.

A narrow Fellow in the Grass
Occasionally rides -
You may have met Him? Did you not
His notice instant is -

The Grass divides as with a Comb -
A spotted Shaft is seen,
And then it closes at your Feet
And opens further on -

He likes a Boggy Acre -
A Floor too cool for Corn -
But when a Boy and Barefoot
I more than once at Noon

Have passed I thought a Whip Lash
Unbraiding in the Sun
When stooping to secure it
It wrinkled And was gone -

Several of Nature's People
I know and they know me
I feel for them a transport
Of Cordiality

But never met this Fellow
Attended or alone
Without a tighter Breathing
And Zero at the Bone.

The editor, Samuel Bowles, had added a title—"The Snake"—to
the poem before publication. As with other poems published by Samuel,
we have no way of knowing whether Emily knew the poem would
be released before she saw it in print. However, in a letter to Thomas

Higginson, Emily made clear she did not approve of the editorial changes made to her work, including modifications of her unusual punctuation that distorted the way the poem was meant to be read. She complained, "The third and fourth [line] were one – I had told you I did not print – I feared you might think me ostensible."

In the early part of 1866, Emily received an invitation from Thomas to meet him in Boston. He had probably read more of her poems than any other person in Emily's life except her sister-in-law, Sue. Yet she and Thomas had never met. Emily wrote back, declining the invitation. She told him that her father strongly disliked her leaving home without him. She added that her father had also refused to let her return to Boston to see her eye doctor, with whom she had a follow-up appointment. Whether this was an excuse to hide her fear of traveling or a legitimate ban from her father, Emily would never again travel from the Homestead. By 1866, she did not leave her house except to go next door to Sue and Austin's house.

In June, a few months later, Higginson again suggested that Emily meet with him in Boston. For the second time, thirty-five-year-old Emily declined. She invited him to Amherst, however.

> 9 June 1866
>
> Dear friend
>
> . . . I must omit Boston. Father prefers so. He likes me to travel with him but objects that I visit.
>
> Might I entrust you, as my Guest to the Amherst Inn? When I have seen you, to improve [my writing] will be better pleasure because I shall know which are the mistakes.
>
> Your opinion gives me a serious feeling. I would like to be what you deem me. . . .
>
> Dickinson.

For the next three years, Emily seemed to be going through a dry period in her creative life. She wrote few new poems or letters between 1866 and 1869, and she had altogether ceased making her fascicles. The exact cause for this slowing is unknown. Some scholars have speculated more ill health in the family. Another theory is that the Dickinson family servant, Maggie, leaving in 1866, not to be replaced until 1869, forced Emily to spend much more of her day on maintaining her father's household and less on writing poetry.

In June 1869, Higginson again invited Emily to visit him. She turned him down again:

> You speak kindly of seeing me. Could it please your convenience to come so far as Amherst I should be very glad, but I do not cross my Father's ground to any House or town.

At last Emily admitted to Higginson that she did not leave her home for any reason. Part of this, as she pointed out in her letters, was her father's dominant control over her life. Although the poet was almost forty years old by 1870, Edward Dickinson still made many major decisions for her and her sister, Vinnie. While Austin had his own wife, children, house, and career, Emily and Vinnie seemed to be stuck in a permanent adolescence in their father's eyes. While the sisters were, at this point, used to Edward's controlling behavior, it made it difficult to assert their autonomy.

Higginson finally took Emily's offer seriously. On August 16, 1870, Emily and Higginson met for the first time. Having read Emily's letters and poetry for eight years, Higginson was eager to meet the remarkable author who wrote with such passion and power. Emily was also curious about what kind of a man her mentor might be.

Higginson expected to find a woman vastly different in appearance and manner from the one he finally met at the Dickinson house. He wrote home to his wife, describing the meeting with Emily, including what she looked like and how she acted.

> I shan't sit up tonight to write you all about E.D. dearest but if you had read Mrs. Stoddard's novels you could understand a house where each member runs his or her own selves. Yet I only saw her.

A large country lawyer's house, brown brick, with great trees & a garden — I sent up my card. A parlor dark & cool & stiffish, a few books & engravings & an open piano. . . . Papers among other books.

A step like a pattering child's in entry & in glided a little plain woman with two smooth bands of reddish hair & a face a little like Bell Dove's; not plainer — with no good feature — in a

POETRY AS THEATER: SHAKESPEARE'S INFLUENCE ON DICKINSON

Few writers are as admired and celebrated as Shakespeare. But although Emily Dickinson read his plays and poetry in her teens, she did not fully embrace the bard until decades later. In the mid-1860s, Dickinson rediscovered Shakespeare and immediately took inspiration from his work. Her poetic output by that point had dwindled, but in her remaining letters and poems, the references to Shakespeare are more pronounced.

One example of a casual, passing reference to Shakespeare in Dickinson's poetry is "A Route of Evanescence," which describes the path of a hummingbird as it goes on its routes of gathering nectar and pollen. The poem closes with "The Mail from Tunis - probably, / An easy Morning's Ride -" The reference is to the capital city of Tunisia, which is featured in Shakespeare's play The Tempest. Dickinson jokingly says the hummingbird is so fast that it could deliver mail to all of Tunis in "An easy Morning's Ride."

Dickinson's love poetry also reveals Shakespeare's influence. She often positions two fated lovers and their pain at not being able to be together—a theme often used in Shakespeare's tragedies. She even placed Shakespeare at the same level in her life as Sue, writing in her last decade,

Dear Sue —

With the exception of Shakespeare, you have told me of more knowledge than any one living — To say that sincerely is strange praise.

very plain & exquisitely clean white pique [dress] & a blue net worsted shawl. She came to me with two day lilies which she put in a sort of childlike way into my hand & said "These are my introduction" in a soft frightened breathless childlike voice — & added under her breath Forgive me if I am frightened; I never see strangers & hardly know what I say . . .

Dickinson's experiments with gender for the speakers of her poems also takes influence from Shakespeare. He frequently used cross-dressing characters in his comedies to create confusion and forbidden romance, as well as using speakers with unidentified gender when writing about seducing or appreciating men. His flexibility of presentation allowed Dickinson to turn her letters and poems into performance rather than strict expression of her own feelings.

Viola (*second from left*) is one of Shakespeare's most famous cross-dressing characters. In *Twelfth Night*, she disguises herself as a male page and becomes entangled in a love triangle with Duke Orsino and Countess Olivia.

Many Dickinson scholars point out her love of performance within writing. She seems, in both letters and poems, to try on different perspectives and masks, never quite pinning down what is her thought and what is imagined. This theatrical form of expression is another piece of her legacy that confuses and entertains, and it may very well be due to her exposure to Shakespeare.

Emily soon lost her shyness and began a conversation with Higginson. But since Emily had not spoken with anyone other than her family members in years, she was out of practice in the social grace that demands that one not monopolize the entire conversation but also give the other person a chance to speak. In the same letter to his wife, Higginson describes Emily's chattiness: "She talked soon & thenceforward continuously – & deferentially – sometimes stopping to ask me to talk instead of her – but readily recommencing."

At the end of the letter, Higginson included part of his conversation with Emily. He quoted her saying:

If I read a book [and] it makes my whole body so cold no fire ever can warm me I know *that* is poetry. If I feel physically as if the top of my head were taken off, I know *that* is poetry. These are the only way I know it. Is there any other way. . . . I find ecstasy in living—the mere sense of living is joy enough.

The following day, Higginson wrote another letter to his wife. It was evident that Emily was still very much on his mind. Higginson also recounted his impression of Emily's father, Edward, based on Emily's description.

Her father was not severe I think but remote. He did not wish them to read anything but the Bible. One day her brother brought home Kavanagh hid it under the piano cover & made signs to her & they read it: her father at last found it & was displeased. . . .

After long disuse of her eyes she read Shakespeare & thought why is any other book needed.

I never was with any one who drained my nerve power so much. Without touching her, she drew from me. I am glad not to live near her. She often thought me *tired* & seemed very thoughtful of others.

At one point, Higginson asked Emily if she ever tired of staying home and not having visitors. She responded by saying that she never thought of "such a want in all future time." Emily seemed happy to be safe in her home, surrounded by the people and things that made her feel safe: her books, pens, paper, and family members.

NINE

I CONFESS THAT I LOVE HIM

1871–1880

As Emily grew older, her creative energy was directed more to letters than poetry. She wrote to her Norcross cousins in Boston, to Elizabeth Holland in New York, and to her sister-in-law whenever Sue was away from Amherst. Emily also continued to write regularly to Higginson.

In November 1871, Emily sent him the following poem—one of her favorites:

> Remembrance has a Rear and Front.
> 'Tis something like a House -
> It has a Garret also
> For Refuse and the Mouse -
>
> Besides the deepest Cellar
> That ever Mason laid -
> Look to it by it's Fathoms
> Ourselves be not pursued -

In the letter that accompanied the poem, she also praised the poems of her old friend Helen Fiske Hunt, whose work she had seen in the *Springfield Daily Republican*. Helen was becoming well known as one of the finest female poets in the country. Emily believed that Helen's poems were stronger than those of any female poet since Elizabeth Barrett Browning.

On July 10, 1872, Edward Dickinson resigned as treasurer of Amherst College. He had held this position for almost forty years, but lately, he had been having periods of ill health and felt the position was too demanding of him.

Emily wrote to Higginson in late 1872, asking him to visit again when he came to Amherst.

To live is so startling, it leaves but little room for other occupations though Friends are if possible an event more fair.

I am happy you have the Travel you so long desire and chastened — that my Master met neither accident nor Death.

> Our own Possessions through our own
> 'Tis well to hoard anew
> Remembering the dimensions
> Of Possibility.

I often saw your name in illustrious mention and envied an occasion so abstinent to me. Thank you for having been to Amherst. Could you come again that would be far better — though the finest wish is the futile one.

When I saw you last, it was Mighty Summer—Now the Grass is Glass and the Meadow Stucco, and "Still Waters" in the Pool where the Frog drinks.

These Behaviors of the Year hurt almost like Music—shifting when it ease us most. Thank you for the "Lesson."

I will study it though hitherto
Menagerie to me
My Neighbor be.
Your Scholar

Emily sent Higginson three poems with her letter: "To disappear enhances," "He preached upon Breadth," and "The Sea said 'Come' to the Brook."

> The Sea said "Come" to the Brook -
> The Brook said "Let me grow" -
> The Sea said "then you will be a Sea -
> I want a Brook - Come now"!

The Sea said "Go" to the Sea -
The Sea said "I am he
You cherished" - "Learned Waters -
Wisdom is stale - to Me" -

On the evening of June 15, 1874, Emily and Vinnie were eating dinner when Austin burst into the house with a telegram in his hand. Their father had collapsed on the floor of the Massachusetts General Court in Boston. Vinnie decided that she would accompany Austin to Boston to be with their father. But by the time Austin and Vinnie had arranged for transportation to Boston to be with their father, they received another telegram saying that Edward Dickinson had died. The news of her father's death was an unexpected shock for Emily. While she had started wearing more plain white dresses in recent years, after his death, she wore only white in mourning for him. Emily wrote to her cousins Loo and Fanny Norcross to share the difficult news. She knew they would understand her pain, since they had lost their mother, Lavinia, a decade earlier.

You might not remember me, dears. I cannot recall myself. I thought I was strongly built, but this stronger has undermined me.

We were eating our supper the fifteenth of June, and Austin came in. He had a despatch in his hand, and I saw by his face we were all lost, though I didn't know how. He said that father was very sick, and he and Vinnie must go. The train had already gone. While horses were dressing, news came he was dead.

Father does not live with us now—he lives in a new house. Though it was built in an hour it is better than this. He hasn't any garden because he moved after gardens were made, so we take him the best flowers, and if we only knew he knew, perhaps we could stop crying. . . .

Emily.

In July, Emily wrote to Higginson, telling him about her last day with her father.

> The last Afternoon that my Father lived, though with no premonition — I preferred to be with him, and invented an absence for Mother, Vinnie being asleep. He seemed peculiarly pleased as I oftenest stayed with myself, and remarked as the Afternoon withdrew, he "would like it to not end."
>
> His pleasure almost embarrassed me and my Brother coming — I suggested they walk. Next morning I woke him for the train — and saw him no more.
>
> His Heart was pure and terrible and I think no other like it exists.
>
> I am glad there is Immortality — but would have tested it myself — before entrusting him.

Emily's relationship with her father was certainly complex. She mourned his loss, but his death also relieved her of his heavy-handed influence on her life. There is also some evidence in Emily's letters and poems to her siblings and friends that Edward controlled his daughter physically as well as mentally. In her groundbreaking book *A Wounded Deer,* published in 2006, Wendy K. Perriman studied whether Emily may have been a survivor of incest by her father. Emily met a startling number of the symptoms many survivors exhibit, and incest could in part explain Emily's mental health issues and her closeness to her siblings, Austin and Vinnie, who could also have been abused. However, like many aspects of her life, Emily's exact relationship with her father can never be definitively answered.

After the death of Emily's father, Judge Otis Phillips Lord visited the Dickinson home several times, and a relationship slowly developed between forty-three-year-old Emily and the sixty-one-year-old judge. Emily had known Mr. and Mrs. Lord almost all her life. Edward Dickinson and Otis had been about the same age. Otis was a judge in Salem, Massachusetts. He was described by a childhood friend as "manly in his deportment, yet not, I am glad to say, without a vein of roguishness. . . . He loved discussion, and the more earnest and excited he was, the more pleasurable it was to him." He also had good common sense and was practical.

Emily greatly admired Otis and began a passionate correspondence with him. The fact that he was married certainly limited their relationship, but the two wrote letters and shared inside jokes. Emily particularly enjoyed Otis's sense of humor. Emily and Otis wrote funny stories on scraps of paper. These scraps flew back and forth from the courthouse in Salem to Emily's writing table in Amherst. One such example reads:

Otis Lord became one of Emily's steadfast correspondents in her later years.

Solomon Pickles: Notice! My wife Sophia Pickles having left my bed and board without just cause or provocation, I shall not be responsible for bills of her contracting.

Sophia Pickles: Notice! I take this means of saying that Solomon Pickles has had not bed or board for me to leave for the last two months.

On June 15, 1875, exactly a year after her father's death, her mother had a stroke and was paralyzed on one side of her body. She also experienced memory problems, forgetting that her husband, Edward, was dead. Emily wrote to Higginson:

Mother was very ill, but is now easier, and the Doctor thinks that in more Days she may partly improve. She was ignorant at the time and her Hand and Foot left her, and when she asks me the name of her sickness—I deceive for the first time. She asks for my Father, constantly, and thinks it rude he does not come— begging me not to retire at night, lest no one receive him. I am pleased that what grieves ourself so much—can no more grieve him. To have been immortal transcends to become so. Thank you for being sorry. . . .

Your Scholar.

Emily's days were spent caring for her mother, doing household chores, tending her garden, writing letters, and reading. When Higginson suggested, in 1876, that he send her poetry to the editor

THE WOMAN IN WHITE: EMILY DICKINSON'S DRESSES

One of the few surviving items we have of Emily Dickinson is a simple white cotton dress, known in its time as a wrapper, or housedress. Simple in its design and made for everyday tasks around the house, the dress is not anything special. But, as with every surviving item that Emily Dickinson touched, it has taken on an air of mystery. Although Emily herself never wrote about wearing exclusively white, it became part of her local mythology. Its sticking power is owed in part to her friend and mentor Thomas Wentworth Higginson, who described in a letter to his wife after he met Emily the childlike, red-haired poet approaching him in her basic white dress and blue shawl, placing flowers in his hand. Mabel Loomis Todd in a letter to her parents also described a woman that "dresses wholly in white" for reasons no one can explain.

As with many rumors, there may have been a grain of truth to these observations. As Emily grew older and stopped leaving Amherst—or even of a women's publication, Emily declined. She did not see the need to make her work public beyond her own sphere of friends, family, and literary peers.

However, Higginson was not the only one pressuring Emily to publish her work. After Higginson told Helen Fiske Hunt about Emily's poetry, Emily and Helen began to correspond with each other. In October 1875, Helen married William S. Jackson, and Emily wrote her a letter of congratulations. Helen Hunt Jackson had become famous, not only as a poet, but as a prose writer as well. When she saw Emily's poems, she felt that more of them should be published. Helen recognized the genius in Emily's poetry and wrote to her:

the Homestead/Evergreens property— she had little reason to dress in the more respectable, colorful daywear for going out. She did not need church clothes, as she did not attend services. In short, there was no compelling reason for her to wear anything other than basic clothing. Housedresses were comfortable, easily bought and repaired, and white dresses in particular were easy to clean.

On the symbolic side, white is seen as the color of marriage, purity, light, and truth. One of Emily's favorite literary characters, Aurora Leigh, also was in the habit of wearing white. Perhaps practicality and a lack of outside social pressures had more to do with Emily's fashion choices than any particular symbolism that scholars have ascribed, but without Emily herself to illuminate us, her choice will continue to be a blank slate onto which new theories can be piled.

I hope some day, somewhere I shall find you in a spot where we can know each other. I wish very much that you would write to me now and then, when it did not bore you. I have a little manuscript volume with a few of your verses in it—and I read them very often—You are a great poet—and it is a wrong to the day you live in, that you will not sing aloud. When you are what men call dead, you will be sorry you were so stingy.

Yours truly

Helen Jackson.

In 1876, Helen wrote to Emily to tell her of a poetry anthology that was to be published. She wanted to see some of Emily's poems in the anthology.

My dear Miss Dickinson,

. . . I enclose to you a circular which may interest you. When the volume of Verse is published in this series, I shall contribute to it: and I want to persuade you to. Surely, in the shelter of such *double* anonymousness as that will be, you need not shrink. I want to see some of your verses in print. Unless you forbid me, I will send some that I have. May I?

An anthology would contain works by several talented poets from around the country. Helen especially wanted Emily to submit a poem that was a personal favorite of hers. The poem was written in Emily's most prolific writing period, the late 1850s and early 1860s. It spoke of the contradictions of success and fame—a fitting reminder of Emily's own complicated views on public recognition.

> Success is counted sweetest
> By those who ne'er succeed.
> To comprehend a nectar
> Requires sorest need.

Not one of all the purple Host
Who took the Flag today
Can tell the definition
So clear of Victory

As he defeated - dying -
On whose forbidden ear
The distant strains of triumph
Burst agonized and clear!

Emily initially declined, but part of her wavered. In a letter to Higginson in October 1876, Emily asked her mentor for advice:

Dear friend —
Are you willing to tell me what is right? Mrs. Jackson — of Colorado — was with me a few moments this week, and wished me to write for this — I told her I was unwilling, and she asked me why? — I said I was incapable and she seemed not to believe me and asked me not to decide for a few Days — meantime, she would write me — She was so sweetly noble, I would regret to estrange her, and if you would be willing to give me a note saying you disapproved it, and thought me unfit, she would believe you — I am sorry to flee so often to my safest friend, but hope he permits me —

The issue lay dormant for the next two years, but Emily and Helen still kept in touch. On October 25, 1878, after a trip to Amherst, Helen wrote to Emily. She urged her friend once again to consider allowing her poem to be published.

My dear Friend —
Here comes the line I promised to send — we had a fine noon on Mt. Holyoke yesterday — and took the 5 o clk train to Springfield. . . .

FAME IS A FICKLE FOOD: EMILY DICKINSON'S POETRY ON POPULARITY

Dickinson's relationship to publication and publicity always seems to hold tension, but the poet was endlessly fascinated by fame and success. She wrote at least a dozen such poems on becoming popular and its effects. The last piece she wrote is also perhaps the most straightforward:

> Fame is a bee.
> It has a song—
> It has a sting—
> Ah, too, it has a wing.

The poem speaks not just to the fickle nature of fame but its emotional power. It "has a song" and "has a sting," with the power to both lift up a writer's spirits or plunge them back down. Other poems recognize the fleeting nature of fame and its habit of following those who don't really want it, as in "To earn it by disdaining it," in which the speaker urges people to ignore fame—it likes rejection, apparently—and instead find joy in their everyday lives instead of relying on fame and success to provide that happiness.

Another piece, "Fame is the one that does not stay" presciently explains that fame clings best to those who are dead or otherwise missing and intangible to a waiting audience. Emily's own role as the mystery of Amherst and the many gaps in her life story seem to follow exactly this blueprint for fame. While that was likely not her intent at that time, Emily nonetheless thrives in our culture precisely because of her many ambiguities—we are enticed by what we do not, and will never, know of her.

Now — will you send me the poem? No — will you let me send the "Success" — which I know by heart — to Roberts Bros for the Masque of Poets? If you will, it will give me a great pleasure. I ask it as a personal favor to myself — Can you refuse the only thing I perhaps shall ever ask at your hands?

Yours ever

Helen Jackson

Emily finally gave her permission. On December 8, 1878, Helen wrote to Emily:

My dear friend,

I suppose by this time you have seen the Masque of Poets. I hope you have not regretted giving me that choice bit of verse for it. I was pleased to see that it had in a manner, a special place, being chosen to end the first part of the volume,— on the whole, the volume is a disappointment to me. Still I think it has much interest for all literary people. I confess myself quite unable to conjecture the authorship of most of the poems. . . .

I am very glad that I saw you this autumn: also that you saw my husband and liked him, as I perceived that you did —

Thank you once more for the verses.

Yours always

Helen Jackson

Emily's poem was published anonymously, like the others in the anthology, and most readers thought "Success" was the work of Ralph Waldo Emerson. No one but Helen Hunt Jackson and Thomas Niles, the publisher of the anthology, knew that it was Emily's poem. On January 15, 1879, Emily received a letter from Thomas Niles.

Dear Miss Dickinson

You were entitled to a copy of "A Masque of Poets" without thanks, for your valuable contribution which for want of a known

A draft of a letter to Otis from 1878

sponsor Mr Emerson has generally had to father.

I wanted to send you a proof of your poem, wh. as you have doubtless perceived was slightly changed in phraseology

Yrs very truly

T. Niles

Unfortunately, Emily also experienced tragedy during this period. In 1877, Samuel Bowles died after a short illness. Higginson's wife, Mary, also died quite suddenly. Both of these deaths affected Emily deeply. But a third death, that of Mrs. Lord, added a new dimension to Emily's life.

By 1878, about a year after Mrs. Lord died, Otis and Emily were writing to each other weekly and sometimes daily. Emily felt safe expressing her most intimate feelings for him. She saved several rough drafts of her letters, all written in 1878:

My lovely Salem smiles at me. I seek his Face so often — but I have done with guises.

I confess that I love him — I rejoice that I love him — I thank the maker of Heaven and Earth — that gave him me to love — the exultation floods me. I cannot find my channel — the Creek turns Sea — at thought of thee —

. . . Don't you know you have taken my will away and I "know not where" you "have laid" it? Should I have curbed you sooner? . . .

. . . to lie so near your longing — to touch it as I passed, for
I am but a restive sleeper and often should journey from your
Arms through the happy night, but you will lift me back, wont
you, for only there I ask to be — I say, if I felt the longing nearer
— than in our dear past, perhaps I could not resist to bless it, but
must, because it would be right. . . .

I was reading a little Book — because it broke my Heart I
want it to break your's — Will you think that fair? I often have
read it, but not before since loving you — I find that makes a
difference — it makes a difference with all.

Emily's letters to Otis were intimate and witty, but she did not share
her poetry with him. He may not have known to what extent poetry was
her life, and he might have been astounded to learn of her prolific writing
habits in decades prior.

Emily and Otis did have a strong connection: their love of
Shakespeare. They eventually used Shakespeare's plays as a kind of
code for cryptic or secret messages in their letters to each other. Most
poetry that Emily wrote during this time of her life was related to her
relationship with Otis. In the following poem, the speaker refers to a love
left dormant for many years that suddenly—brightly—burns. It seemed
Emily might have always felt deep emotions for Otis that in "a second"
were stirred into passionate love.

> Long Years apart - can make no
> Breach a second cannot fill -
> The absence of the Witch does not
> Invalidate the spell -
>
> The embers of a Thousand Years
> Uncovered by the Hand
> That fondled them when they were Fire
> Will stir and understand

TEN

BLOW HAS FOLLOWED BLOW

1880–1890

n 1880, the love affair between Otis and Emily Dickinson was still very strong. At one point, Otis is said to have proposed to the poet, who playfully declined. The judge tried to visit Amherst when he could, but as with many people in Emily's life, they also communicated strongly by letter. Through their correspondence, their intimacy grew. Emily again poured out her heart to Otis:

> [I kissed the little blank — you made it on the second page you may have forgotten —] I will not wash my arm — the one you gave the scarf to — it is brown as an Almond — 'twill take your touch away. . . .
>
> It is strange that I miss you at night so much when I was never with you — but the punctual love invokes you soon as my eyes are shut — and I wake warm with the want sleep had almost filled — I dreamed last week that you had died — and one had carved a statue of you and I was asked to unvail it — and I said what I had not done in Life I would not in death when your loved eyes could not forgive —

But this time was not without sadness. In late 1882, she wrote, "Blow has followed blow, till the wondering terror of the Mind clutches what is left. . . .Some of the hardest blows were to come: Her nephew, Gilbert "Gib" Dickinson, died in 1883 at just eight years old. Otis died a year later in March 1884. It was a crushing loss for Emily. With her parents and lover gone and her remaining family in mourning, Emily sunk into a deep depression.

It wasn't long before the emotional traumas that Emily had experienced impacted her already fragile health. Emily's family had always closely guarded against illness, but the poet had been frail and prone to poor health for much of her adult life. In June 1884, Emily collapsed in the kitchen while baking a cake.

> I was making a loaf of cake with Maggie, when I saw a great darkness coming and knew no more until late at night. I woke to find Austin and Vinnie and a strange physician bending over me, and supposed I was dying, or had died, all was so kind and hallowed. I had fainted and lain unconscious for the first time in my life. Then I grew very sick and gave the others much alarm, but am now staying [alive]. The doctor calls it "revenge of the nerves"; but who but Death had wronged them?

After her collapse, Emily wrote a poem about her fear of her inevitable death. She compared death to a child approaching a hill. The child, not knowing what was on the other side, was excited and scared to discover it. The poem asks whether finding the answer to this great mystery is worth the fear of facing death alone.

> The going from a world we know
> To one a wonder still
> Is like the child's adversity
> Whose vista is a hill,
> Behind the hill is sorcery
> And everything unknown,
> But will the secret compensate
> For climbing it alone?

By November 1885, fifty-four-year-old Emily was spending most of her time in bed. She was suffering from kidney disease and high blood pressure, which can cause heart disease. On the days when she felt well, she wrote letters to her cousins, Higginson, and several surviving friends.

ONE-WAY TRIP: ANALYZING "BECAUSE I COULD NOT STOP FOR DEATH"

In her most prolific writing period of 1861 to 1863, Emily Dickinson wrote an average of almost a poem a day. Among those poems lay what would become one of the most famous poems in the English language. At six stanzas of four lines each, "Because I could not stop for Death" is one of Dickinson's longer poems. The stanzas are known as quatrains, from the Greek root for four. The poem personifies Death as a gentleman stopping to pick up the speaker for a carriage ride during which she realizes her fate. It reads:

Because I could not stop for Death -
He kindly stopped for me -
The Carriage held but just Ourselves -
And Immortality.

We slowly drove - He knew no haste
And I had put away
My labor and my leisure too,
For His Civility -

We passed the School, where Children strove
At Recess - in the Ring -
We passed the Fields of Gazing Grain -
We passed the Setting Sun -

Or rather - He passed Us -
The Dews drew quivering and Chill -
For only Gossamer, my Gown -
My Tippet - only Tulle -

We paused before a House that seemed
A Swelling of the Ground -
The Roof was scarcely visible -
The Cornice - in the Ground -

Since then - 'tis Centuries - and yet
Feels shorter than the Day
I first surmised the Horses' Heads
Were toward Eternity -

In the first stanza, we learn the initial idea of the poem—the speaker
and Death going on a carriage ride—as well as adapt to the fairly strict
meter and rhyme. The rhyme scheme is every other line, with a different
rhyme for each stanza. Dickinson uses ballad meter, a favorite of hers,
and almost always follows the rules of the form. Ballad meter alternates
between iambic tetrameter and iambic trimeter. This means the first and
third lines of each stanza have eight syllables and those syllables follow
the unstressed / stressed / unstressed / stressed pattern. For instance, the
opening line is scanned, or analyzed for meter, as follows:

be / CAUSE / i / COULD / not / STOP / for / DEATH

We can quickly see the line breaks down into eight beats, but iambic
rhythm can be a little harder to find. The key is to emphasize the second
syllable in each pair, so "because" reads as "be-CAUSE." It almost sounds
like horses running, with their second step coming down harder than the
first. As for iambic trimeter, it follows the same unstressed / stressed
pattern, but there are only six syllables in each line.

The second stanza establishes the seeming politeness of Death and
the speaker. They are in no rush, and the speaker has stopped her other
tasks for as long as Death wants her. She does not yet realize how long
that will be. The third stanza introduces elements of the world the speaker
is unknowingly leaving behind. Children are playing, crops are staring
outward, the sun begins to set. The next stanza has the speaker realize it
isn't she who is moving, but the rest of the world—the sun passes her, not
the other way around, and its absence chills her in her thin, ghostlike dress
and sheer cape. The surprise is registered in the meter, which Dickinson flips
for the first two lines of the fourth stanza. Instead of the regular eight then
six meter lines, she uses six then eight as a way to startle her readers out
of the familiar rhythm.

The final two stanzas have the speaker fully realize where she has been headed all along. In the fifth stanza, the speaker passes a "House" that is buried up to the ceiling in the earth, not yet understanding this underground house is her final resting place. The last stanza reveals it is not just the speaker that was unaware. She turns the joke on us, admitting she has been dead and buried for hundreds of years, but she remembers the journey and her discovery of her death as if it were yesterday.

The poem includes many of the hallmarks of Dickinson's work—ballad meter and musicality, imperfect rhyme schemes, unusual metaphors, an emphasis on death and nature, and a slight manipulation of the reader's expectations. It also makes heavy use of dashes, her signature punctuation, even ending on a dash. This refuses to give the poem the closure a period would, further defying the conventional form of the day. But even if readers don't have experience with poetry or Dickinson before reading the poem, it makes an impact anyway. Such is the talent of Dickinson.

When the spring of 1886 was ushered in, Emily was too ill to read or write. In one of her last letters to Higginson, she wrote: "I have been very ill, Dear friend, since November, bereft of Book and Thought."

On May 13, 1886, Emily went into a coma. She never regained consciousness, and she died on May 15, with Vinnie and Austin by her side.

The funeral was held in the Homestead with friend and mentor Thomas Higginson and the closest members of the Dickinson family. In a tribute to Emily, Higginson read a poem about immortality by Emily Brontë. It was one of Emily's favorites and was the last poem Brontë wrote.

> No coward soul is mine,
> No trembler in the world's storm-troubled sphere:
> I see Heaven's glories shine,
> And Faith shines equal, arming me from Fear.
>
> O God within my breast,
> Almighty, ever-present Deity!
> Life, that in me has rest
> As I, undying Life, have power in Thee!
>
> Vain are the thousand creeds
> That move men's hearts: unutterably vain; Worthless as
> withered weeds,
> Or idleist froth amid the boundless main,
>
> To waken doubt in one
> Holding so fast by Thy infinity,
> so surely anchored on
> The steadfast rock of Immorality.
>
> With wide-embracing love
> Thy Spirit animates eternal years,
> Pervades and broods above,

Changes, sustains, dissolves, creates, and rears.

Though earth and moon were gone,
And suns and universes ceased to be,
And Thou wert left alone,
Every existence would exist in Thee.

There is not room for Death,
Nor atom that his might could render void:
Since Thou art Being and Breath
And what Thou art may never be destroyed.

After the eulogy, Vinnie placed two heliotropes in Emily's hands "to take to Judge Lord," and the coffin was closed forever.

On May 18, Emily's obituary was printed in the *Springfield Daily Republican*. In a moving testament to a life that defied conventional milestones of a woman in 1800s Massachusetts, Sue Gilbert Dickinson wrote:

The death of Miss Emily Dickinson, daughter of the late Edward Dickinson, at Amherst on Saturday, makes another sad inroad on the small circle so long occupying the old family mansion. It was for a long generation overlooked by death, and one passing in and out there thought of old-fashioned times, when parents and children grew up and passed maturity together, in lives of singular uneventfulness unmarked by sad or joyous crises. Very few in the village, excepting among the older inhabitants, knew Miss Emily personally, although the facts of her seclusion and her intellectual brilliancy were familiar Amherst traditions. . . .

Her talk and her writings were like no one's else, and although she never published a line, now and then some enthusiastic literary friend would turn love to larceny, and cause a few verses surreptitiously obtained to be printed. . . .

Emily Dickinson is buried at West Cemetery in Amherst alongside her grandparents, parents, and sister.

Her swift poetic rapture was like the long glistening note of a bird one hears in the June woods at high noon, but can never see. Like a magician she caught the shadowy apparitions of her brain and tossed them in startling picturesqueness to her friends, who, charmed with their simplicity and homeliness as well as profundity, fretted that she had so easily made palpable the tantalizing fancies forever eluding their bungling, fettered grasp. . . .

To her life was rich, and all aglow with God and immortality. With no creed, no formulated faith, hardly knowing the names of dogmas, she walked this life with the gentleness and reverence of old saints, with the firm step of martyrs who sing while they suffer. How better note the flight of this "soul of fire in a shell of pearl" than by her own words? —

Morns like these, we parted;

Noons like these, she rose;

Fluttering first, then firmer,

To her fair repose.

A few weeks after Emily's death, Vinnie found a locked chest in Emily's room. Upon opening it, Vinnie found her sister's poetry, either bound in fascicles or written on an odd assortment of paper scraps, from envelopes to the backs of recipe cards.

Vinnie felt that these poems should be shared with the world. She asked Sue to help her get them published. But Sue had a different vision of how Emily's work should be made public. Sue wanted to lay out all of Emily's letters and poetry chronologically, showing her life and relationships in their entirety. But Vinnie, after waiting two years for Sue to finish her version of the book, decided she could wait no longer.

Next, Vinnie turned to Mabel Loomis Todd. The choice was unconventional, as Mabel had for years been having a not-so-hidden affair with Sue's husband and Emily's brother, Austin. But Mabel was also a writer and was very excited to be part of such a worthy project. Vinnie needed someone with enthusiasm to take on the gargantuan task of sorting through Emily's nearly eighteen hundred poems and corralling them into some kind of sensible order. Mabel probably didn't know that it would be such a time-consuming endeavor, but she stayed committed to the project.

Emily's handwriting was difficult to decipher, and she used an odd style of punctuation in both her letters and poetry. Mabel spent many hours and days rewriting or typing hundreds of poems, organizing them according to theme (as was common at the time), and trying to get them published. Mabel also went a step further in her editing by changing many aspects of Emily's writing. Some modifications were seemingly harmless and had been done by editors before her, such as Samuel Bowles. Mabel standardized Emily's incorrect and inconsistent spellings and introduced different punctuation and line breaks. She also titled many of the poems to better fit the conventions of the day, with the help of collaborator Thomas Higginson.

But Mabel Loomis Todd also undoubtedly brought an agenda to her editing. As one might expect, Mabel did not much care for her lover Austin's wife, Sue. She saw Sue as cold and undeserving of Austin, lost in her grief over Gib's and Emily's deaths. One of the most consistent changes Mabel made was to systematically erase, blot out, or literally scrape from the page many references to Sue in Emily's letters to her other correspondents. She

A COMPLEX LEGACY:
THE LIFE OF MABEL LOOMIS TODD

She is best remembered as either the hardworking, heavily revisionist editor of Emily's poetry or the scandalous mistress of Austin Dickinson, but there is much more to Mabel Loomis Todd than meets the eye. Born in 1856 to Mary "Molly" Wilder and Eben Loomis, Mabel's childhood was a lonely one. She was an only child, and her parents, determined to keep her from spending time with anyone of lower social standing, homeschooled her. Mabel also grew up in the midst of the Civil War and was just nine years old when President Abraham Lincoln was assassinated in 1865.

After the war, Eben decided to try his hand at managing a cotton plantation, which quickly failed, then moved to Washington, DC, where Molly and Mabel would join him a few years later. The Loomis family would end up living in boardinghouses (not all that uncommon at the time) and moving often to get by. Oddly enough, Mabel's family finances mirrored those of Sue Gilbert's, although Mabel's parents remained alive. Mabel, like Sue, split her time between different states with different family members. In Mabel's case, she stayed part of the year in Concord, Massachusetts, with her grandparents and part in the nation's capital with her father. In both places, Mabel thrived on the praise and attention of adults, as well as the flirtatious advances of scores of local boys.

It was back in the Washington, DC, social scene that Mabel caught the eye of David Todd. The wealthy, well-bred astronomer encouraged Mabel's artistic passions, including writing, singing, playing piano, and drawing. He was also very much in love with her and didn't seem to mind when other men found her attractive. The pair were married in 1879. Their first and only daughter, Millicent, was born the following year. In 1881 David accepted an astronomy teaching job at his alma mater, Amherst College, and the newlyweds set off for Amherst. Mabel left her infant daughter Millicent with her parents in Concord. Millicent would end up spending much of her childhood there, separate from her parents.

As someone used to the bustling social scene of Washington, DC, Mabel was afraid small-town life in Amherst would be unbearably boring and uneventful. Thankfully for her, Susan Dickinson was still holding her literary salons and parties with public figures. Mabel quickly grew attached to Sue and her three children, spending nearly every day over at the Evergreens. She spent so much time there that Ned, the oldest Dickinson son at twenty and only five years Mabel's junior, quickly fell in love with the glamorous, flirtatious woman from out of town. Mabel did little to discourage his advances, and it wasn't until she fell for Ned's father in 1882 that she cut Ned off completely. She remained close friends with Sue and Mattie until Ned shared his suspicions about Mabel and Austin's relationship.

Despite Mabel and Austin's early attempt to keep their affair a secret, it was not long before all of Amherst was sharing this new juicy gossip. The couple did not break things off after being found out, though—far from it. Over the next thirteen years, the pair wrote hundreds of letters back and forth, much of which they couldn't bear to burn and kept hidden but close. Austin and Mabel believed their love fated, a kind of once-in-a-generation, star-crossed-lovers' romance that superseded little things such as the fact that they were both married with children. David, for his part, actively encouraged his wife's affair. Since Austin was the treasurer of Amherst College, he could negotiate David's salary, and David had a lifelong habit of unfaithfulness himself.

Austin and the Todds' decision to embrace the affair left Sue and the Dickinson sisters in an uncomfortable predicament. Sue still begged her husband to end the affair and work on their marriage, but Vinnie secretly helped her older brother organize trysts at the Homestead, just out of sight of his wife. Emily was often too ill to protest and likely was not aware of the drama unfolding in her own family.

After Austin's death in 1895, Mabel went into public mourning—an unusual choice for a woman whose husband was very much alive. She also kept up her work on Emily's poems and letters and became a speaker and self-proclaimed local expert on the poet. In the twentieth century, Mabel would travel the world with her husband and daughter, then return to give lectures on scientific and literary topics. She survived the tense, drawn-out court battle over land Austin had promised her but Vinnie refused to give her rights to, and she was out of the grip of Amherst. Mabel died in 1932, leaving her daughter, Millicent, to carry on her work and defend her legacy.

Mabel Loomis Todd exchanged letters with Emily Dickinson, but never met the poet in person.

also carefully left out passages of Emily's letters referring to Sue in glowing, loving terms, and removed dedications of poems to Sue.

In some cases, Mabel actually tried to destroy poems of Emily's that clearly expressed her affection for Sue, such as her inking over the (then) only known copy of "One Sister have I in our house." If not for the recovery of another copy of the poem in letters held outside Mabel's control, the poem might never have come to light. For these reasons, scholars are still trying to piece together what letters and poems may have been censored early on and if they can recover words that were intentionally removed.

Other edits were subtler, but ultimately more impactful, on how Emily's poetry was received. Mabel and Higginson occasionally substituted words to better fit a rhyme or meter. These changes would not be fully recognized until R. W. Franklin combed through all the paperwork associated with the years of work Mabel poured into the editing process. He identified minute instances where language was changed, providing Dickinson scholars with—in his view—the first "true" collection of Dickinson's poetry.

Despite her mixed motivations, Mabel is one of the main reasons Emily's poetry reached a wider audience. She approached Higginson to help select the first poems for publication, since she knew that Emily and Higginson had had a long relationship. He agreed, selecting a few hundred poems from the collection that he felt were worthy of publication. He and Mabel approached publisher after publisher in an attempt to get Emily's poems into print. But they all rejected the idea, saying that her poetry was too odd for public taste.

Eventually, one publisher agreed to print 116 of her poems, but he wouldn't pay for the production costs, so Vinnie paid for them out of her own pocket. Mabel herself designed the drawing of the Indian Pipes flower (one of Emily's favorites) that adorned the cover. In 1890 the first volume of Emily Dickinson's poems was published, titled simply *Poems*. All 408 copies sold within a few months, and the public clamored for more. Several editions were printed over the next few years, and more collections of Emily's poems were published.

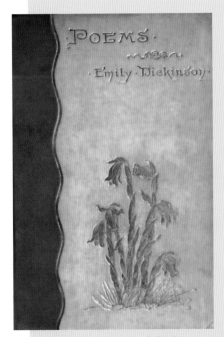

The first volume of Emily Dickinson's poems was a critical and financial success; the book went through eleven printings in two years.

It wasn't until 1955 that all 1,775 of her known poems were published, and in 1958, the existing letters—more than 1,050 of them— were published. Adding the letters that Vinnie had destroyed, the volume of correspondence that Emily had engaged in during the fifty-five years of her life was staggering. At the end of her life, Emily wrote the following poem:

> A Letter is a joy of Earth -
> It is denied the Gods -

ELEVEN

TELL ALL THE TRUTH BUT TELL IT SLANT

1890–2020

Emily Dickinson is far from the only writer to become famous after death. However, from the moment her poetry was prepared for publication, her legacy became a topic of debate. Soon, battle lines were drawn between the surviving Dickinsons and Todds. Lavinia began to resent Mabel for becoming, in effect, the face of Emily's poetry.

To promote the first volume of *Poems*, Mabel gave talks at literary salons and reading groups, agreed to newspaper and journal interviews, and sent the book to many prominent writers of the day who she thought might appreciate the unusual, daring style of Emily's work. This hard work of marketing such an odd project would be appreciated by modern publishers, but for Vinnie, Mabel's efforts seemed to be a stealing of her sister's memory. To further complicate matters, Austin's death in 1895 resulted in a dramatic, drawn-out trial over a piece of land.

He had willed land to his sister Vinnie, but he had promised his mistress Mabel that Vinnie would turn over the land to Mabel and her daughter, Millicent, after his death. This would avoid the impropriety of having their affair in the public record but still ensure Mabel got a piece of Austin's holdings and would be able to live near the Dickinson family with whom she had such a complicated relationship. However, Vinnie refused to hand over the land and—when the matter went to court—won her case to the horror of Mabel.

Bitter about Vinnie's sudden about-face, and having given years of her life to editing, publishing, and marketing Emily Dickinson's letters and poetry, Mabel had had enough. She stopped work on Emily's poetry and letters and locked the remaining hundreds

of poems in a chest. There they would stay, untouched, for decades. Finally, with the centennial of Emily's birth approaching and with Mabel's own health rapidly failing, a new Todd would step in to take up the mantle of publication.

Millicent Todd Bingham, Mabel Loomis Todd's only child, already had her own life and career following her father, David, into science. But her mother begged Millicent to carry on the work of publishing the remaining poetry and letters Mabel had kept buried for so long. Millicent reluctantly agreed, knowing the work would put her own career ambitions on hold and take years (eventually, decades) of her time. She took a lighter editorial hand than her

Mabel Loomis Todd (*left*) asked her daughter, Millicent Todd Bingham (*right*), to assist her in publishing Emily Dickinson's remaining letters and poems. However, Mabel died shortly thereafter, in 1932, and Millicent continued the work alone.

mother, but she still had to bow to convention in order to get Emily's work into the world. She published her first collection of Emily's poems in 1945, and by 1955 had published the last of her store in several other volumes.

While Millicent was hard at work with her half of the Dickinson papers, another loyal daughter was finishing her mother's mission. Martha Dickinson Bianchi, only daughter of Susan and Austin Dickinson and niece of Emily Dickinson, had inherited her mother's private collection of letter-poems sent from the house next door. Mattie, as she was called by her parents and doting aunt, was determined that the Todds would not be the ones to build Emily Dickinson's legacy.

To that end, she worked tirelessly not just to publish new, revealing letters and poetry between her mother and her aunt, but to actively shape the public image of Emily. It was Mattie who helped establish the idea of Emily as a virginal recluse in white, playful yet childish. Mattie suggested Emily's later shunning of attention from all but her closest family and friends resulted from a great lost love, sparking the debate over the mystery man for the ensuing decades. She also helped revive interest in her aunt's poetry with a brand-new collection of poems titled *The Single Hound* in 1914.

In her most well-known book, *Emily Dickinson Face to Face*, published in 1932, Mattie included many anecdotes she remembered from her mother or from her own dealings with the poet. In this, Mattie had a distinct advantage—unlike Mabel and Millicent, Mattie had met Emily, as she put it, face-to-face. This gave her accounts added weight, even though they were skewed in an attempt to shape public opinion of the Dickinson clan. Scholars continue to value Mattie's books, mixed as they are with letters and memoir, truth and fiction, for their firsthand insight into Emily's life.

Now came the challenging piece: What to do with the manuscripts? Millicent had been Mabel's only child, and she herself did not have children. Mattie was similarly childless and unmarried, having divorced her husband in 1920. Mattie eventually willed her portion of the Dickinson letters and poetry to her editing assistant Alfred Leete Hampson. Hampson and his wife, Mary, also took charge of the Evergreens property, with Mary finally bequeathing it to the Emily Dickinson Museum after her death. Hampson made the decision to sell the Dickinson collection to Harvard University in 1950. To this day, the original manuscripts that Lavinia and

In addition to editing and publishing her aunt's poems and letters, Martha Dickinson Bianchi was a poet and wrote several novels.

Susan once possessed are in a special library on Harvard's campus.

Representatives from Harvard quickly approached Millicent Todd Bingham about her half of the manuscripts, hoping to get all of Emily's work under one roof. But despite firm—and in some cases, outright bullying—tactics, Millicent refused. Instead, she willed her collection to the institution Emily's grandfather Samuel had founded: Amherst College. The college later helped establish the Emily Dickinson Museum by purchasing the Homestead and filling the old house with the surviving pieces of furniture and other effects of Emily's. Though all direct descendants of Edward and Emily Dickinson are dead, as are all the original Todds, the feud between these two houses lives on.

REDISCOVERING DICKINSON: FEMINIST AND QUEER ANALYSIS OF THE POET

Emily Dickinson's life and poetry had long been popular, but in the 1970s, some interest started to fade. Thomas Johnson had published his definitive collection of Emily's poetry in the 1950s, complete and in the "right" order chronologically, and all those who knew the poet personally were dead. But second-wave feminism and queer theory breathed unexpected new life into Emily Dickinson scholarship.

In a feminist reading of Emily's life and poetry, one sees a woman repressed by conventional standards of poetry, a woman's role in nineteenth-century New England, and her family's tight hold on the poet. Where earlier studies found a sad, dejected Dickinson, feminist scholars saw anger set loose in violent poems with bright imagery. Her unconventional spellings, punctuation, and overall style sought to undermine the misogynist choke hold of her day, pushing past the limits of what women "should" do. Queer theory likewise dug into her choices, finding in her unconventional use of gender and style a queer, flexible viewpoint that informed her poetic voice.

Emily Dickinson has been a treasured American poet for more than a century. She has been compared to several other trailblazing writers of the nineteenth century, including Walt Whitman, Henry David Thoreau, and her hero, Elizabeth Barrett Browning. Her poetry has a permanent place in the American literary canon and is taught in schools and universities around the world. But something about Emily has also captured imaginations of those outside the literary world, drawing them into her mystery.

Perhaps one factor in that fascination is the jagged, unusual publication path that Emily's letters and poems went through, as well as their continued revisions since as scholars work to undo the editorial efforts of Mabel, Mattie, Millicent, and others. Another is the many gaps in Emily's story. She was elusive even to those who knew her in life, and

Both feminist and queer theory also helped recenter the role of women in Emily's life instead of fixating on mysterious male suitors. In perhaps the earliest known book calling out Emily's potential queerness, *The Riddle of Emily Dickinson* by Rebecca Patterson claimed a romantic connection between Emily and a friend of Sue's, Kate Anthon (also known as Catherine Turner). While in 1951 the world was not ready to see a beloved American writer as gay, Patterson's work helped open a door to rethinking Emily's life and identity. Other writers such as Ellen Louise Hart and Martha Nell Smith, authors of *Open Me Carefully* in 1998, dug deeper into the expectations and obscured facts of the poet's life.

As these new theories and methods of reading literature arrived on college campuses, Dickinson became a frequent subject. There was so much unknown about her life and poems that they lent themselves well to endless interpretations. The largest contributions of feminist and queer theory to Emily's story is in the freedoms of fresh perspective that they allowed students and scholars to take. New articles did not have to agree with those that came before—almost everything was negotiable and up for debate. Emily Dickinson still provides a wealth of material for everyone to study, as evidenced by the *Emily Dickinson Journal* that has been published twice a year for every year since 1991. There is no end to the discovery.

in death she became even more so. And of course, hidden romance or speculation thereof is a potent motivator for public interest. Because Emily herself gives so few clear answers to the facts of her life and poetry, readers can fill in the gaps with their own theories and story lines.

Pop culture in particular is fascinated with the possibilities of Emily's love life. One of the earliest takes on Emily after her death and publication was actually a rather racy play in which Emily tries to seduce fellow 1800s writer Helen Hunt Jackson's husband as Helen stands by, scandalized. Two twenty-first-century takes on Emily's life, the film *Wild Nights with Emily* and the TV show *Dickinson*, both embrace an Emily Dickinson who is unabashedly sexual and queer, having relationships with Sue Gilbert as well as men in her life.

Other depictions of Emily's life and work have instead focused on the themes of her poetry to guide them. The 2017 film *A Quiet Passion* delved into the darker themes of death, mental health, and undercurrents of violence in Emily's poems. However, it also fell back on some of the outdated ideas of Emily as trapped, alone, and loveless. A one-woman play that premiered in 1976 included, in essence, dramatic readings of many of Emily's letters and poetry, revealing their musicality and rhythms that are easier understood out loud.

One surprising outlet for adaptation has been music. Emily's poetry does follow strong rhythms, and her work can be performed to several popular songs and hymns. But musical compositions go far beyond just setting her words to a basic tune. Her poetry has inspired operatic-style performances, string quartets, and full orchestral arrangements that draw on the themes of certain poems.

Despite all the other artistic avenues Emily Dickinson's life and work have inspired, the most lasting and interesting is the impact she made on poetry. Many writers of prose and poetry have cited Emily Dickinson as an early inspiration that made them fascinated with language. Poet and essayist Susan Howe dedicated an entire book—*My Emily Dickinson*—to her relationship with the poet. Others, like Paul Legault, have opted for a more playful approach. In Legault's *The Emily Dickinson Reader*, all of Emily's nearly eighteen hundred poems are reduced to pithy one-liners that often incorporate humor and modern language. Respected American fiction writer Joyce Carol Oates created a curated volume of her own favorite Dickinson poems, remembering with fondness her early love for the poet. Emily's daring form helped pave the way for free verse and poetry that revels in creative shapes on the page.

Emily's poems are accessible to a wide range of audiences in a way that the work of many other highly revered poets is not. Her poems are short, melodic, and catchy. They lend themselves as well to memorization as to in-depth study. And because of the sheer quantity of poems and letters she produced, there are always new pieces to discover. It is no wonder, then, that she continues to captivate the imaginations of readers across the globe, inviting them in to her mysterious world.

THAT'S A FACT!
DICKINSON, EPISODE 2: CHESTNUTS AT THE VESPER BELL

In the show, Sue and Austin each eat a chestnut at the ring of the vesper bell, which signaled the start of evening religious services known as vespers. Emily quickly ruins the moment, declaring she'll eat one at the same time. Sue and Austin did actually eat chestnuts at the vesper bell as their own secret ritual in the earliest stages of their courtship, unbeknownst to Emily or anyone else.

THAT'S A FACT!
DICKINSON, EPISODE 3: VINNIE AND JOSEPH LYMAN

In episode 3, Lavinia sits on the lap of her crush, Joseph Lyman, and ties her hair around his neck. This outspoken, undeniably flirty gesture is something Vinnie did in real life, and she was never subtle or ashamed of her behavior with him. She started trying to get Joseph's attention when she was just thirteen, and he responded in kind until she was eighteen and actually marriageable, at which point he broke things off and moved out of state.

SORRY, WHAT?
DICKINSON, EPISODE 10: THE WEDDING

In the finale of Dickinson's first season, Emily is seen pouting in her room as her brother, Austin, and sister-in-law, Sue, get married downstairs. The only problem is, Austin and Sue's wedding took place in New York, far from the Dickinson Homestead. For that reason, there was no way Emily could have disturbed the wedding. She was two states away at the time!

THAT'S A FACT!
A QUIET PASSION: NO HOPE AT MOUNT HOLYOKE

Early in this biopic, a young Emily refers to herself as a "No-Hoper," using the actual term for nonreligious students created by Mary Lyon, the founder and head of Mount Holyoke Female Seminary while Emily was at school there. She was definitely not the only one, but she stood out to Mary and the other teachers as a soul in particular need of help to be "saved,"

SORRY, WHAT?
A QUIET PASSION: VRYLING BUFFAM

Throughout *A Quiet Passion*, Vinnie's friend Vryling Buffam rails against the tyranny of men, only to get married herself later in the film. She is offhanded, snarky, and witty. One thing she isn't? A real person. Writer and director Terence Davies invented this character completely for the movie, and Vinnie never had a friend that scholars can find acted similarly to Vryling.

THAT'S A FACT!
WILD NIGHTS WITH EMILY: RECIPE POEMS

In *Wild Nights*, Emily gives a poem to Sue that is written on the back of a recipe. Dickinson did do quite a bit of writing in the kitchen, as is evidenced by the poem scraps found on recipes, the backs of food packaging, and other assorted bits and bobs she could find. It's also true that Emily sent writing to Sue very frequently throughout their lives, sometimes enlisting Sue's children to deliver little notes, poems, and letters.

SORRY, WHAT?
WILD NIGHTS WITH EMILY: MARTHA DICKINSON BIANCHI'S EMILY

Near the end of the film, Martha Dickinson Bianchi, Sue's daughter, is seen trying to promote her own book on Emily's life that provides a new role for her mother, Sue, as incredibly important to Emily. While it's true that Mattie's books did give a broader role to Sue in Emily's life, Mattie was just as responsible, if not more responsible, than Mabel Loomis Todd for positioning Emily as a loveless recluse. It was Mattie who started the theory that Emily descended into seclusion after an unrequited love in her mid-twenties and that she never loved again. She saw nothing at all unusual or romantic in her mother's relationship with Emily, despite having all of their letters at her disposal.

SOURCES

5 Emily Dickinson, "I'm Nobody! Who are you?," in *The Poems of Emily Dickinson*, ed. R. W. Franklin (Cambridge, MA: Belknap, 1999), 116–117.

9–10 Richard B. Sewall, *The Life of Emily Dickinson* (Cambridge, MA: Harvard University Press, 1980), 324.

10 Sewall, 74.

11 Cynthia Griffin Wolff, *Emily Dickinson* (New York: Knopf, 1986), 62.

13 *Primary Education Vol. 16* (Boston: Educational, January 1908), 223.

14 Dickinson, " 'Hope' is the thing with feathers," in *The Poems of Emily Dickinson*, 140.

21 Emily Dickinson to Austin Dickinson, April 18, 1842, in *The Letters of Emily Dickinson*, ed. Thomas H. Johnson (Cambridge, MA: Belknap, 1958), 1:3–4.

24 Dickinson to Jane Humphrey, April 18, 1842, in *The Letters of Emily Dickinson*, 1:6–7.

25–26 Dickinson to Abiah Root, February 23, 1845, in *The Letters of Emily Dickinson*, 1:9–11.

26–27 Dickinson to Root, May 7, 1845, 1:12–14.

27 Dickinson to Thomas Higginson, April 25, 1862, in *The Letters of Emily Dickinson*, 2:404.

27 Arnold B. Cheyney, *Legends of the Arts: 50 Inspiring Stories of Creative People* (Tucson: Good Year Books, 2007), 35.

28 Dickinson to Root, May 7, 1845, 1:13.

29 Dickinson to Root, March 28, 1846, 1:32.

33 Dickinson, " 'Nature' is what We see," in *The Poems of Emily Dickinson*, 322.

34 Dickinson, "It's all I have to bring today," in *The Poems of Emily Dickinson*, 26.

37 Dickinson to Root, January 31, 1846, 1:27–28.

39 Dickinson, "The Bumble of a Bee," in *The Poems of Emily Dickinson*, 99–100.

39 Dickinson to Root, 1:27.

40 Dickinson, "I felt a Funeral, in my Brain," in *The Poems of Emily Dickinson*, 153.

40 Dickinson, "Dying! To be afraid of thee," in *The Poems of Emily Dickinson*, 402.

40–41 Dickinson, "I never felt at Home - Below," in *The Poems of Emily Dickinson*, 202.

41 Dickinson to Austin Dickinson, South Hadley, October 21, 1847, 1:47–49.

42–44 Dickinson to Root, South Hadley, November 6, 1847, 1:53–56.

44 Dickinson to Austin Dickinson, South Hadley, October 21, 1847, 1:48.

45 Mary Lyon, *Mary Lyon: Documents and Writings*, ed. James E. Hartley (South Hadley, MA: Doorlight, 2008), 382.

48 Dickinson to Root, South Hadley, November 6, 1847, 1:55.

49 Dickinson to Root, South Hadley, May 16, 1848, 1:65–67.

50 "Mount Holyoke and the New Century," Mount Holyoke College, accessed October 19, 2021, https://ascdc.mtholyoke.edu/exhibits/show/woolleymarks /5202.

50 "Mount Holyoke."

51 Dickinson to Root, 1:66–67.

51 Dickinson, "I went to thank Her," in *The Poems of Emily Dickinson*, 285.

55 Dickinson to Root, May 7 and 17, 1850, 1:97–99.

59 Dickinson to Austin Dickinson, June 8, 1851, 1:111–112.

59 Dickinson to Austin Dickinson, October 1, 1851, 1:136.

59 Dickinson to George H. Gould, February 1850, in *The Letters of Emily Dickinson*, 1:91.

60 Dickinson to Gould, 1:92.

60 George H. Gould, "Editor's Corner" in the *Indicator*, February 7, 1850.

61–62 Dickinson to Susan Gilbert (Dickinson), March 1853, in *The Letters of Emily Dickinson*, 1:226.

62 Dickinson, "Sic transit gloria mundi," in *The Poems of Emily Dickinson*, 17–18.

62 Dickinson, "On this wondrous sea - sailing silently," in *The Poems of Emily Dickinson*, 19.

63 Dickinson to Susan Gilbert (Dickinson), March 1853, 1:226.

63 Dickinson to Susan Gilbert (Dickinson), January 15, 1854, 1:283–284.

64 Dickinson to Susan Gilbert (Dickinson), 1:284.

64 Dickinson to Susan Gilbert (Dickinson), 1:284.

64 Dickinson to Susan Gilbert (Dickinson), 1:283–284.

65, 67 Sewall, *The Life of Emily Dickinson*, 165.

69 Dickinson to Root, March 14, 1847, 1:45.

71 Dickinson to Susan Gilbert (Dickinson), February 6, 1852, 1:175–176.

73 Dickinson to unknown recipient, 1861, in *The Letters of Emily Dickinson*, 2:373–375.

74 Dickinson to Susan Gilbert (Dickinson), February 1852, 1:177.

76 Dickinson to Susan Gilbert Dickinson, 1858, 2:344.

82 Dickinson to Elizabeth Holland, Philadelphia, March 18, 1855, in *The Letters of Emily Dickinson*, 2:318–319.

83–84 Dickinson to Elizabeth Holland, January 20, 1856, 2:323–324.

84 Sewall, *The Life of Emily Dickinson,* 8.

85 Dickinson to John Graves, April 1856, in *The Letters of Emily Dickinson*, 2:327–328.

87 Martha Ackmann, "The Encounter That Revealed a Different Side of Emily Dickinson," *Atlantic*, June 23, 2020, https://www.theatlantic.com/culture/archive/2020/06/day-emily-dickinson-met-thomas-wentworth-higginson/613357/.

90 Dickinson, "One Sister have I in the house," in *The Poems of Emily Dickinson*, 21.

94 Dickinson, "I taste a liquor never brewed," in *The Poems of Emily Dickinson*, 96.

94–95 Dickinson to Susan Gilbert Dickinson, 1861, 2:379.

95 Dickinson to Susan Gilbert Dickinson, 1861, 2:379.

95 Susan Gilbert Dickinson to Emily Dickinson, 1861, in *The Letters of Emily Dickinson*, 2:379–380.

97 Martha Dickinson Bianchi, *The Life and Letters of Emily Dickinson* (New York: Houghton Mifflin, 1924), 14.

98 Dickinson to Higginson, April 25, 1862, 2:404.

98 Dickinson, "What would I give to see his face?," in *The Poems of Emily Dickinson*, 118–119.

100 Dickinson, "The Moon is distant from the Sea," in *The Poems of Emily Dickinson*, 178.

100–101 Dickinson, "South winds jostle them," in *The Poems of Emily Dickinson*, 55.

101 Dickinson, "The Malay - took the Pearl," in *The Poems of Emily Dickinson*, 208.

101 Dickinson, "No matter - now - Sweet," in *The Poems of Emily Dickinson*, 327–328.

101 Dickinson, "Wild nights - Wild nights!," in *The Poems of Emily Dickinson*, 120–121.

101 Dickinson to Higginson, April 15, 1862, 2:403.

101 Dickinson to Higginson, April 25, 1862, 2:404.

104 Dickinson to Higginson, 2:404–405.

104 Dickinson to Higginson, 2:404.

105 Dickinson, "Dear March - Come in," in *The Poems of Emily Dickinson*, 510–511.

108 Dickinson, "Some keep the Sabbath going to Church," in *The Poems of Emily Dickinson*, 106.

108 Dickinson, "Blazing in Gold and quenching in Purple," in *The Poems of Emily Dickinson*, 143.

109 Dickinson to Lavinia Dickinson, Cambridge, 1864, in *The Letters of Emily Dickinson*, 2:430.

109 Dickinson to Higginson, Cambridge, June 1864, 2:431.

110 Dickinson to Louise "Loo" Norcross, 1865, in *The Letters of Emily Dickinson*, 2:438–439.

111 Richard B. Sewall, "The Lyman Letters," *Massachusetts Review* 6, no. 4 (Autumn 1965): 772.

113 Dickinson, "A narrow Fellow in the Grass," in *The Poems of Emily Dickinson*, 443–444.

114 Dickinson to Higginson, 1866, 2:450.

114 Dickinson to Higginson, June 9, 1866, 2:453–454.

115 Dickinson to Higginson, June 1869, 2:460.

115–117 Thomas Higginson to Mary Higginson, Amherst, August 16, 1870, in *The Letters of Emily Dickinson*, 2:473.

116 Dickinson, "A Route of Evanescence," in *The Poems of Emily Dickinson*, 559.

116 Dickinson to Susan Gilbert Dickinson, 1882, 3:733.

118 Higginson to Mary Higginson, 2:473.

118 Higginson to Mary Higginson, 2:473–474.

118 Higginson to Mary Higginson, Amherst, August 17, 1870, 2:475–476.

119 Dickinson to Higginson, Amherst, August 16, 1870, 2:474.

121 Dickinson, "Remembrance has a Rear and Front," in *The Poems of Emily Dickinson*, 485.

122 Dickinson to Higginson,1872, 2:500–501.

122–123 Dickinson, "The Sea said 'Come' to the Brook," in *The Poems of Emily Dickinson*, 497.

123 Dickinson to Louisa "Loo" Norcross and Frances "Fanny" Norcross, 1874, in *The Letters of Emily Dickinson*, 2:526.

124 Dickinson to Higginson, July 1874, 2:528.

124–125 Sewall, *The Life of Emily Dickinson*, 650.

125 Bianchi, *The Life and Letters of Emily Dickinson*, 70.

125–126 Dickinson to Higginson, July 1875, 2:542.

126 Sewall, *The Life of Emily Dickinson*, 216.

128 Helen Hunt Jackson to Dickinson, Colorado Springs, CO, March 20, 1876, in *The Letters of Emily Dickinson*, 2:545.

128 Jackson to Dickinson, Princeton, NJ, August 20, 1876, 2:563.

128–129 Dickinson, "Success is counted sweetest," in *The Poems of Emily Dickinson*, 59.

129 Dickinson to Higginson, October 1876, 2:562–563.

129, 131 Jackson to Dickinson, October 25, 1878, 2:625.

130 Dickinson, "Fame is a bee." in *The Poems of Emily Dickinson*, 635.

131 Jackson to Dickinson, Colorado Springs, CO, December 8, 1878, 2:626.

131–132 Thomas Niles to Dickinson, January 15, 1879, in *The Letters of Emily Dickinson*, 2:626.

132 Dickinson to Otis Lord, 1878, in *The Letters of Emily Dickinson*, 2:615.

132 Dickinson to Lord, 1878, 2:616.

133 Dickinson to Lord, 1878, 2:617.

133 Dickinson, 535.

133 Dickinson, "Long Years apart - can make no," in *The Poems of Emily Dickinson*, 535.

135 Dickinson to Lord, 1880, 3:663–664.

135 Dickinson to Holland, December 1882, 3:754.

136 Dickinson to Louise "Loo" Norcross and Frances "Fanny" Norcross, August 1884, 3:826–827.

136 Dickinson, "The going from a world we know," in *The Poems of Emily Dickinson*, 601.

137–138 Dickinson, "Because I could not stop for Death," in *The Poems of Emily Dickinson*, 219–220.

139 Dickinson, 220.

140 Dickinson to Higginson, 1886, 3:903.

140–141 Emily Brontë, *The Complete Poems of Emily Jane Brontë*, ed. C. W. Hatfield (New York: Columbia University Press, 1941), 243–244.

141 Jay Leyda, *The Years and Hours of Emily Dickinson* (Hamden, CT: Archon Books, 1970), 475.

139 Dickinson, 220.

141–142 Susan Gilbert Dickinson, "Miss Emily Dickinson of Amherst," *Springfield (MA) Daily Republican*, May 18, 1886, https://www.emilydickinson.it/edobituary.html.

147 Dickinson, "A Letter is a joy of Earth," in *The Poems of Emily Dickinson*, 604.

SELECTED BIBLIOGRAPHY

WORKS BY EMILY DICKINSON

Dickinson, Emily. *The Complete Poems of Emily Dickinson: With an Introduction by Her Niece, Martha Dickinson Bianchi*. Boston: Little, Brown, 1924.

————. *The Complete Poems of Emily Dickinson*. Edited by Thomas H. Johnson. Boston: Little, Brown, 1960.

————. *Emily Dickinson: Selected Letters*. Edited by Thomas H. Johnson. Cambridge, MA: Belknap, 1971.

————. *Letters of Emily Dickinson*. Edited by Mabel Loomis Todd. 2 vols. Boston: Robert Brothers, 1894.

————. *The Letters of Emily Dickinson*. Edited by Thomas H. Johnson and Theodora Ward. 3 vols. Cambridge, MA: Belknap, 1958.

————. *The Master Letters of Emily Dickinson*. Edited by R. W. Franklin. Amherst, MA: Amherst College Press, 1986.

————. *Poems: Selections*. Edited by Mabel Loomis Todd and T. W. Higginson. Boston: Robert Brothers, 1890.

————. *The Poems of Emily Dickinson: Including Variant Readings Critically Compared with All Known Manuscripts*. Edited by Thomas J. Johnson. 3 vols. Cambridge, MA: Belknap, 1955.

OTHER SOURCES

Bennett, Paula. *Emily Dickinson, Woman Poet*. Iowa City: University of Iowa Press, 1990.

Bianchi, Martha Dickinson. *The Life and Letters of Emily Dickinson: By Her Niece, Martha Dickinson Bianchi*. Boston: Houghton Mifflin, 1924.

Chase, Richard. *Emily Dickinson*. New York: Sloane, 1951.

Dobrow, Julie. *After Emily: Two Remarkable Women and the Legacy of America's Greatest Poet*. New York: W. W. Norton, 2018.

Farr, Judith. *The Gardens of Emily Dickinson*. With Louise Carter. Cambridge, MA: Harvard University Press, 2004.

————. *The Passion of Emily Dickinson*. Cambridge, MA: Harvard University Press, 1992.

Garbowsky, Maryanne M. *The House without the Door*. Rutherford, NJ: Fairleigh Dickinson University Press, 1989.

Gordon, Lyndall. *Lives like Loaded Guns: Emily Dickinson and Her Family's Feuds*. New York: Viking, 2010.

Habegger, Alfred. *My Wars Are Laid Away in Books: The Life of Emily Dickinson*. New York: Random House, 2001.

Hart, Ellen Louise, and Martha Nell Smith. *Open Me Carefully: Emily Dickinson's Intimate Letters to Susan Huntington Dickinson*. Ashfield, MA: Paris, 1998.

Johnson, Thomas H. *Emily Dickinson: An Interpretative Biography.* Cambridge, MA: Belknap, 1955.

Linscott, Robert N., ed. *Selected Poems and Letters of Emily Dickinson.* New York: Doubleday, 1959.

Lombardo, Daniel. *Tales of Amherst.* Amherst: University of Massachusetts Press, 1986.

Longsworth, Polly. *Austin and Mabel: The Amherst Affair and Love Letters of Austin Dickinson and Mabel Loomis Todd.* New York: Farrar, Straus & Giroux, 1984.

Lundin, Roger. *Emily Dickinson and the Art of Belief.* 2nd ed. Grand Rapids, MI: William B. Eerdmans, 2004.

Messmer, Marietta. *A Vice for Voices: Reading Emily Dickinson's Correspondence.* Amherst: University of Massachusetts Press, 2001.

Miller, Cristanne. *Emily Dickinson: A Poet's Grammar.* Cambridge, MA: Harvard University Press, 1987.

Mitchell, Domhnall. *Emily Dickinson: Monarch of Perception.* Amherst: University of Massachusetts Press, 2000.

Pollak, Vivian, ed. *A Poet's Parents.* Chapel Hill: University of North Carolina Press, 1988.

Sewall, Richard B. *The Life of Emily Dickinson.* Cambridge, MA: Harvard University Press, 1980.

Todd, Mabel Loomis. *Letters of Emily Dickinson.* New York: Harper & Brothers, 1931.

Walsh, John Evangelist. *The Hidden Life of Emily Dickinson.* New York: Simon and Schuster, 1971.

Whicher, George. *This Was a Poet.* Amherst, MA: Amherst College Press, 1992.

Wineapple, Brenda. *White Heat: The Friendship of Emily Dickinson and Thomas Wentworth Higginson.* New York: Knopf, 2008.

Wolff, Cynthia Griffin. *Emily Dickinson.* New York: Knopf, 1986.

Wolosky, Shira. *Emily Dickinson: A Voice of War.* New Haven, CT: Yale University Press, 1984.

FURTHER READING

BOOKS

Ackmann, Martha. *These Fevered Days: Ten Pivotal Moments in the Making of Emily Dickinson*. New York: W. W. Norton, 2020.
Using archival letters, poems, and photos, take a deep dive into ten crucial days in the life of Emily Dickinson.

Bronski, Michael. *A Queer History of the United States for Young People*. With Richie Chavet. Boston: Beacon, 2019.
Discover and celebrate the accomplishments of LGBTQ figures throughout American history.

Currey, Mason. *Daily Rituals: Women at Work*. New York: Alfred A. Knopf, 2019.
Read about the choices Emily Dickinson and 142 other women creatives made and continue to make for their art.

Goddu, Krystyna Poray. *Becoming Emily: The Life of Emily Dickinson*. Chicago: Chicago Review Press, 2019.
Find out more about Emily Dickinson's journey to becoming a poet in this accessible biography.

McDowell, Marta. *Emily Dickinson's Gardening Life: The Plants and Places That Inspired the Iconic Poet*. New York: Timber, 2019.
Following a year in Emily Dickinson's garden, this book weaves together letters, poems, and art to explore how Dickinson's deep passion for plants informed and inspired her writing.

Midorikawa, Emily, and Emma Claire Sweeney. *A Secret Sisterhood: The Literary Friendships of Jane Austen, Charlotte Brontë, George Eliot, and Virginia Woolf*. Boston: Houghton Mifflin Harcourt, 2017.
Vibrant friendships of literary women throughout history are highlighted through letters and diary entries in this book.

Wind, Lee. *No Way, They Were Gay? Hidden Lives and Secret Loves*. Minneapolis: Zest Books, 2021.
This book examines primary source letters, poems, and more to rethink the lives and loves of historical figures.

WEBSITES

Emily Dickinson Museum
https://www.emilydickinsonmuseum.org/
The museum is located on the Homestead and Evergreens properties and provides programming and resources related to Emily Dickinson and her family.

"Overlooked No More: Charlote Brontë, Novelist Known for *Jane Eyre*"
https://www.nytimes.com/2018/03/08/obituaries/overlooked-charlotte-bronte.html
Read the *New York Times* obituary for Charlotte Brontë, part of the paper's series on remarkable people whose deaths originally went unreported.

Poetry Foundation: Emily Dickinson
https://www.poetryfoundation.org/poets/emily-dickinson
Read about Emily Dickinson's impact on American poetry, as well as a history
of her life and the publication of her works.

MULTIMEDIA WORKS

"Bloom — is Result — to meet a Flower": Dickinson's Flowering Favorites with Marta
McDowell
https://www.emilydickinsonmuseum.org/past-virtual-programs-archive/
Marta McDowell, author of *Emily Dickinson's Gardening Life*, delves into how the
flowers and other plants in the poet's garden relate to her poetry.

Emily Dickinson's Bedroom Virtual Tour
https://roundme.com/embed/Bqnj2GvyxPJQISHK94bm
See the bedroom where Emily Dickinson lived and wrote for many years.

Filreis, Al. "Amplitude and Awe: A Discussion of Emily Dickinson's 'Wild
Nights - Wild Nights!' and 'She rose to His Requirement.'" *Poem Talk.*
April 15, 2015. https://www.poetryfoundation.org/podcasts/76942/amplitude
-and-awe-a-discussion-of-emily-dickinsons-wild-nights-wild-nights-and-she
-rose-to-his-requirement.
This podcast consists of a close reading and roundtable discussion of the poems
"Wild nights — Wild nights!" and "She rose to His Requirement."

Finding Emily Dickinson in the Power of Her Poetry
https://www.themorgan.org/exhibitions/emily-dickinson
Learn more about the 2017 Emily Dickinson exhibition put on by the Morgan
Library and Museum in New York City.

My Letter to the World. Directed by Sol Papadopoulos. Liverpool, UK: Hurricane Films,
2017.
This documentary inspects the life of Emily Dickinson and challenges the
long-held narrative of the reclusive woman in white.

INDEX

PHOTO ACKNOWLEDGMENTS

Image credits: Bettmann/Getty Images, pp. 1, 42; Visions of America, LLC/Alamy
Stock Photo, p. 4; Houghton Library, Harvard University, Cambridge, MA, pp. 5, 15,
65; Wikimedia Commons (Public Domain), pp. 8, 147; Laura Westlund/Independent
Picture Service, pp. 9, 83, 88–89; Culture Club/Getty Images, pp. 10, 20; Library
of Congress/Corbis/VCG/Getty Images, p. 13; The Archives & Special Collections at
Amherst College/Wikimedia Commons (Public Domain), p. 21; Amherst College Archives
& Special Collections, pp. 23, 71, 73, 90, 132; SSPL/Getty Images, p. 31; Houghton
Library © President and Fellows of Harvard College, pp. 32, 87; Wendy Maeda/The
Boston Globe/Getty Images, p. 35; AS400 DB/Getty Images, p. 39; Heritage Art/
Heritage Images/Getty Images, p. 47; Todd-Bingham Picture Collection (MS 496E).
Manuscripts and Archives, Yale University Library, pp. 54, 94, 125, 150; University of
Leeds Library/Wikimedia Commons (Public Domain), p. 55; © Todd-Bingham picture
collection/Yale Collection: Manuscripts and Archives, p. 82; Edward Wilton Carpenter,
Charles Frederick Morehouse/Wikimedia Commons (Public Domain), p. 85; Amherst
College Archives & Special Collections/The Jones Library, p. 97; Universal History
Archive/Getty Images, p. 103; Niday Picture Library/Alamy Stock Photo, p. 110;
The Picture Art Collection/Alamy Stock Photo, p. 117; Photo courtesy of the Emily
Dickinson Museum, pp. 127, 151; AP Photo/Beth Harpaz, p. 142; Mabel Loomis Todd.
Todd-Bingham Picture Collection (MS 496E). Manuscripts and Archives, Yale University
Library/Wikimedia Commons (Public Domain), p. 146.

Cover: Amherst College Archives & Special Collections.